MASONIC SPEECH MAKING

MASONIC
SPEECH MAKING

J. W. Hobbs

London
A LEWIS (Masonic Publishers) LTD

First published 1971
Second edition 1974
Third edition 1979

ISBN 0 85318 055 9

MADE AND PRINTED IN GREAT
BRITAIN BY THE GARDEN CITY PRESS
LIMITED LETCHWORTH,
HERTFORDSHIRE SG6 1JS

CONTENTS

INDEX TO CONTENTS

An easy reference to any subject, speech, Toast, or reply. (Speeches and Replies are numbered to assist selection).

* Indicates a Reply is given as well as a Speech.

* Indicate a Reply is given as well as a Speech.

PREFACE

IT IS A well-known and widespread experience that Masonic speeches, in general, have resolved themselves into set forms, without variations, hackneyed in terms, and tiresome to the hearer and unsatisfactory to the speaker. To some extent this arises from the almost invariable nature of the occasions when speeches are required in Lodge or elsewhere, and is more noticeable, perhaps, in proposing or replying to Toasts and other after-dinner interludes. Possibly speakers have acquired the habit of imitating the language of their predecessors and contented themselves in so doing, with the reflection that it has saved them working up a speech. The result in any case of this kind is one many deplore, especially listeners; many seek to avoid but fail for various reasons; but many more need guidance in form and language, and suggestive ideas, to enable them to speak more freely and without wearisome iteration.

Oratory is an inborn talent in but few individuals, while with most it is an acquired art—the result, indeed, of application and practice. To the least able, some advantage will accrue by preparation; the most able know that this is the secret of their success. The finest speeches or orations have always been carefully prepared beforehand. Many pains have been taken to make the language apt and appealing, and in all cases the results always justify, and are equal to, the effort made.

The speeches and addresses given follow a general arrangement or classification. They can be utilised in whole or part as may be selected or needed. This is specially so in regard to personal or individual circumstances, local knowledge, custom, and the like. If longer speeches than those given are wanted, additional remarks can be obtained from other examples, or two or more may be combined, special care being given to make the result appropriate and coherent.

The greater number require but little change of mode of address, name, title or rank to be available not only for the Craft, but the Royal Arch, Mark or other Degrees where such are not specially provided.

As a final word, let me advise every reader or utiliser of this book to select examples within his own scope, or that of his audience. To exercise judgment in amending, amplifying or selecting, and, above all, to practise what he intends to use. Practise without fail—aloud, if convenient, for that will give confidence, while knowledge will produce expertness, and obviate hesitation, repetition or poorness of ideas. As far as possible, speak from notes, or without them. Avoid reading a speech if possible, but if you must read it, do so openly, for furtive glances at your manuscript and hesitation over the continuity, caused by losing your place, are worse than the effect of reading. But even reading requires practice and attention in order to make the address vigorous and life-like. An apparently extempore speech is always far more effective. Beware of long speeches in general. A good, but short speech is more effective and interesting than a poor long one. The former will be most welcome to your audience and will reflect credit on yourself and be a valuable example to others.

J. WALTER HOBBS.

1

IN BY-GONE TIMES

*Feasting a Craft Custom from Early Days—Old Lodge
and After-Lodge Customs—Old Masonic Toasts and Music*

FROM the earliest days of Grand Lodge down to the
present time a dinner has followed the Quarterly
Communication of that body. For example, the Minutes
for 24th June, 1721, record: "After Grace said, they sat
down in the ancient manner of Masons to a very elegant
feast and dined with joy and gladness."

The first Book of Constitutions which was issued in 1723
states: "You may enjoy yourselves with innocent Mirth,
treating one another according to Ability, but avoiding all
Excess or forcing any Brother to eat or drink beyond his
Inclination or hindering him from going where his Occasions
call."

Even before the advent of a Grand Lodge, however, in
the period when Operative Freemasonry was merging into
Speculative, it was customary for the brethren to take
refreshment together.

Elias Ashmole, referring to a Lodge meeting in a note
in his Diary in the year 1682, wrote: "We all dined at
the Half Moon Tavern in Cheapside, at a noble dinner
prepared at the charge of the new accepted Masons."
Again in 1686, Dr. Plot referred to a "Collation" being
provided previous to the admission of Freemasons.

Apparently, sometimes the meal preceded the work,
sometimes it followed, and possibly the custom of having
a meal, and latterly a feast, arose from the fact that in the
early days many of the brethren had to travel considerable
distances on foot or on horseback to attend a Lodge meeting.

The first Grand Lodge was formed at a meeting held in
a tavern at which the "Four Old Lodges" took part. This

was the Goose and Gridiron in St. Paul's Churchyard, and meetings continued to be held in taverns until 1721. Engraved Lists of the Lodges were first issued in 1723, and the first one contained a list of fifty-one Lodges, forty-seven of which met at taverns, and the other four met at coffee houses, where the sale of liquid refreshment was not limited to the beverage that the name would imply. The Engraved List for 1725 gave particulars concerning sixty-two Lodges, all but three of which met at taverns. To-day, in London, many Lodges meet on licensed premises termed Hotels or Restaurants, but in the provinces and abroad a number of Masonic Temples or Halls have been built to provide the necessary accommodation. In the eighteenth century it was customary to describe a Lodge as "The Brethren meeting at . . . Arms."

However, even in the early days, there were some Lodges who met in a hall or on their own premises. *The Old Dundee Lodge, No. 18, was one, and for the "Annual Feast," which corresponds to our Installation Banquet of to-day, for St. John the Baptist's Day, 24th June, 1749, the following expenses are recorded :—

1749, June 24, Expences.

	£	s.	d.		£	s.	d.
6 Ducks . . .		8	0		3	3	6
2 Necks of Veal		6	0	Beans, 6 Qts. Pease			
1 Ham . . .		8	6	6 Qts. . .		6	0
Wine . . .	1	5	0	Colliflowers — Cabbages . .		1	0
Rum, Lemons —				Bread, Sauce, etc. .		9	0
Sugar . .		8	6	Dressing . . .		5	0
Beer — Tobacco		7	6	French Horns (Musick) . .		10	6
				Tarts . . .		7	6
				Tyler . . .		2	6
				Servants . . .		2	6
	£3	3	6		£5	7	6

* "Ancient Freemasonry and the old Dundee Lodge, No. 18," by Arthur Heiron.

Ten members were present, also eight visitors who paid 2s. 6d. each, and two visitors from "St. Johns" who paid nothing but gave the "Musick."

A sumptuous meal for twenty persons at a cost which might well arouse the envy of the brethren of the present day.

Bro. Arthur Heiron, the author of the History of this Lodge, records therein : "It is clear that up to 1763 our Brethren were allowed not only to smoke in Lodge, but also to eat and drink, porter being the favourite beverage in their early days ; light refreshments would be supplied, most likely bread and cheese and sandwiches, as only one dinner a year was allowed—i.e. the 'Annual Feast.' When, however, the Lodge improved in status and removed, in 1763, to our own freehold building (No. 20), Red Lion Street, Wapping, a higher tone was introduced into our proceedings, and as the fumes of porter were now thought objectionable, wine was in future regularly provided."

In those early days the ceremonies were much more simple than they are to-day, and the members generally met in a room in a tavern which to-day would be termed the Club Room. Sand would be swept away from the door, and it was the duty of the Tyler to draw the Lodge (Tracing Board) on the floor, and after the ceremony the candidate, with mop and pail, cleaned the drawing off the floor.

The brethren then seated themselves around trestle tables, and the education (masonic) of the candidate was proceeded with by means of question and answer which we to-day term the Lectures.

Bro. Arthur Heiron records that in connection with the Old Dundee Lodge in 1790, "Thirty yards of bordered green cloth were purchased to cover same (the tables) with, and on these tables were placed the bowls of steaming punch, bottles of wine, rum, Hollands, brandy, sugar, lemons, nutmeg, and glasses ; and for the smokers 'churchwardens,' screws of tobacco (called 'papers'), and pipe lights were supplied; it being remembered that smoking and drinking were also allowed in Grand Lodge for many years." The Minutes of the Old Dundee Lodge for 23rd October, 1788, record that "The Members of the Old Dundee Lodge having this Night been presented with an Elegant china Bowl by Dr. Baverstock, they returned him Publick and Sincere Thanks by Drinking his Health with Three Times Three." *

To Dr. Desaguliers is attributed the revival of the custom of drinking toasts in 1729, and this practice in the olden days was frequently accompanied by the singing of songs. We find some of these in old Masonic books, e.g. Cole's "Ancient Constitutions" of 1721; "Ahiman Rezon" the Constitutions of the Antients, published in 1760, etc., and to-day we, perhaps too infrequently, hear sung "The Master's Song," "The Warden's Song," and the "Entered Apprentice's Song." Chorus songs were also sung by the brethren in unison, e.g. "Rule Britannia," "Hearts of Oak," "This Day a Stag must Die," "Wine Cannot Cure," "What Folly Boys to be Downhearted."

As has been stated, toasts were introduced, but not speeches, and at certain periods when "Question and Answer" was in course of procedure, a toast was introduced by the Master. Thus, in the Lectures, we get a reminiscence of this, as for example "The heart that conceals and the tongue that never reveals."

The health of the newly-admitted member was drunk in formal manner, and the reply was probably equally formal, and dictated to him by the Deacon.

Our pleasurable habit of dining together dates back to the custom of the old Gilds, to the era of the earliest days of the great Cathedral Builders, and it forms no insignificant part of Masonry to-day. Our practice of speech-making is of later origin, and it can materially assist towards the

* Note similarity to modern "Fire."

desirable attainment of "being happy and communicating happiness," and at the same time of imparting some worthwhile knowledge so that "profit and pleasure" may be the result.

2

NOTES ON USE OF SPEECHES

THE speeches given are prepared mainly to be delivered by Brethren in and after Lodge, and can appropriately be used by the highest to the lowest in Masonic rank.

The mode of address should be adapted as the circumstances require.

It is not necessary to name Brethren by their Degrees, i.e. "W.M., P.M.s, Wardens, Officers, and Brethren," but only the W.M. or any Brother specially honoured.

For other than Craft Degrees, remember to use the correct title of the Degree and of Officers and Brethren, and the like. To avoid repetition, there are but few speeches specially directed to other Degrees.

Few indications or mention of a personal nature are given. These vary with every Lodge and every Brother. Such as are given are for guidance. Add where suggested or elsewhere any particulars of Lodge or local history, details or personal merit, services and the like.

Compare speeches of a somewhat similar character and use part or parts to add to the completeness of your intended speech. Thus compare speeches of congratulation with those of presentation, and so on.

Make up your mind beforehand in good time. Decide on your selection, and any variations, and do not, except for good cause, alter it. Do not leave these matters to the last moment.

Some practice will be needful, and advisable, so as to obtain good results. Hurry may lead you to obvious or ludicrous results.

Finally, read, and be guided by, the Preface.

3

PLANNING THE PROGRAMME

The Toast List—Allotting Speeches—Preparing Time Table—Seating—Grace—Absent Brethren

ON Installation Night, when the new Master has been duly installed and has invested his officers, and the usual Masonic business is concluded with the closing of the Lodge, the task of the new Master has, in a sense, only just begun. If he is wise he will have considered the matter carefully beforehand, and arrived at some sort of plan.

The programme, that is the toast list, generally follows a set arrangement. In London Lodges the toast list is usually as follows :—

The Queen and the Craft

———

The M.W. the Grand Master

———

The M.W. the Pro. Grand Master, the R.W. Deputy Grand Master, and the rest of the Grand Officers, Present and Past

———

Brethren of London Grand Rank

———

The Master

———

The Immediate Past and Installing Master

———

The Visiting Brethren

———

The Past Masters and Officers of the Lodge

———

The Tyler's Toast

19

If, during his year, the Master is "going up for" one of the Institutions or the Hospital, then an appropriate toast may be introduced if a distinguished brother representing one of those institutions is present by special invitation ; and, of course, he replies to the toast.

In the provinces the toast list is similar except that "Brethren of London Grand Rank" is replaced by "Deputy Provincial Grand Master and the Provincial Grand Officers, Present and Past," this being preceded by "The R.W. the Provincial Grand Master."

The toasts of "The Queen and the Craft" and "The Grand Master" are generally better given by the Master without comment. Probably on Installation Night at least, he will consider it his duty to propose the toast of the "Grand Officers" himself, also that of "Immediate Past and Installing Master," and "The Past Masters and Officers of the Lodge." This leaves a certain number of other toasts, and the replies, to be arranged for, and if the proceedings are to be really profitable, it is well to give as much warning as possible to those who will be called upon to speak. It is difficult to do this in connection with replies to the "Visitors" toast, but in all other cases it is generally possible, and a letter should be sent to the brethren selected a few days before the meeting, thus giving them the opportunity of preparing what they propose to say.

If musical items are to be introduced they should be carefully planned and arranged. From the above list of toasts, on the assumption that each but the first two toasts and reply thereto will occupy seven minutes, and allowing two replies to the "Officers" toast, and three for the "Visitors" the actual speech-making will take from about fifty minutes to an hour. Therefore, if, for example, dinner is called for 7 p.m. and it will probably be 8.30 before it is over, one hour for the speeches would make the time 9.30 p.m. leaving, say, one hour, for music, if the meeting is to conclude with the "Tyler's" Toast at 10.30 p.m.

Probably someone will be a little long winded, and, of course, those present desire to have some opportunity to talk together and not to have to sit quiet listening to speech and song in rapid succession.

The Master will probably find it an advantage to prepare a time table, and with his watch on the table in front of him will be able to see how the proceedings are going and use discretion in the matter of encores.

Thus :—

Dinner	7 p.m.
The Queen and Craft	8.30 p.m.
The Grand Master	8.35 p.m.
Give Brethren permission to smoke	
G.L. Officers' Toast	8.40 p.m.
G.L. Officers' Reply	8.45 p.m.
Song	8.50 p.m.
Encore	8.55 p.m.
Toast to Absent Brethren	9 p.m.
Toast to L.G.R. or Prov. G. Officers	9.5 p.m.
Reply to L.G.R. or Prov. G. Officers	9.10 p.m.
Song	9.15 p.m.
Toast of W.M.	9.20 p.m.
Reply of W.M.	9.25 p.m.
Song	9.30 p.m.
Encore	9.35 p.m.

etc., etc.

If the programme is behind the time table the encores can be eliminated, and if required allowed later in the evening.

It should not be overlooked that there is music and song appropriate to the Craft, e.g. "The Master's Song," "The Entered Apprentice's Song," "The Warden's Song," which date back some years, while if the toast of "Absent Brethren" is observed at 9 o'clock, the introduction of an appropriate hymn after the toast is pleasing, as is that of singing the National Anthem after the Loyal Toast. An appropriate song to precede the toast of "The Initiate" is the poem, "The Arrow and the Song" set to music. There are also appropriate poems by that eminent poet and Freemason Rudyard Kipling, e.g., "Banquet Night," "The Palace," "My Mother Lodge," "My New Cut Ashlar," and "The Thousandth Man."

In many Lodges it is customary to observe certain toasts, during the meal, by the Master taking wine with various brethren. The list of these toasts should be prepared beforehand either by the I.P.M. or the Master, and this pleasing custom should be used with reason and discretion to avoid undue disturbance of the comfort of those present. For example, if the Master takes wine with his officers, it is unnecessary to do so also with them individually.

The question of preparing speeches is referred to in another chapter, so it may be assumed here that the Master has prepared the speeches he is going to make, has notified other speakers, arranged his musical programme, and advised Bro. Director of Ceremonies and Bro. Organist of his plans.

Seating at the tables is generally entrusted to the Director of Ceremonies or his assistant. The Master, by custom, sits at the centre of the top table, and the I.P.M. takes the place on his immediate left. Next to the I.P.M. comes the Chaplain, or a senior P.M. and others follow according to seniority. The Initiate should be placed on the immediate right of the Master, and next to him G.L. officers in order or rank, then Provincial officers or Brethren of London Rank. The S.W. takes the head of the cross table on the right, the J.W. the head of that on the left, while if there are other cross tables or legs, the positions at the head are generally occupied by the Treasurer, Secretary, D.C. or Almoner.

The Master's guests can be conveniently placed on the centre leg or cross table, as near to him as possible, and the wise Master will acquaint Bro. D.C. of the number of guests he is bringing so that the arrangement for their seating may be made.

Care should be taken to ensure that undue time is not lost in the interval between leaving the Lodge and going into dinner. Remember the meal has been ordered to be prepared by a stated time, and it does not improve by delay.

When the brethren have assembled at the tables, and after they have been called to order by the D.C. and the Master has taken his seat, his first duty is to sound the gavel and say Grace. A very usual custom is to use the Latin form of Grace, "Benedictus, Benedicat" (May the Blessed One Bless), before the meal, and "Benedicto, Benedicatur" (May the Blessed One be Blessed) after the meal.

In March, 1933, Lord Ampthill, in addressing those present at the Quarterly Communication of Supreme Grand Chapter, expressed his personal dissatisfaction with the use of a Latin form of Grace by an Institution not having connection with Monastic or Academic Institutions from which such forms of Grace were derived. Their use suffers further from the fact that a number of brethren. do not understand the meaning of the words.

A form of Grace in English which is often used is "For What we are About to Receive may the G.A.O.T.U. give us Grateful Hearts"; this, however, gains an increased appeal if the following words are added : "And keep us mindful of the needs of others."

The Grace after the meal which Lord Ampthill used on the occasion already referred to, was, "For this refreshment of body and mind, let us be thankful to the Giver of all good things."

In some Lodges, of course, it is the custom to sing Grace after the meal, in which case the necessary time has to be devoted to it and considered in planning the programme.

Grace after the meal having been said or sung, it is wise, so soon as the D.C. or Bro. Tyler has sent the waiters outside the room, for the Master to give the toast of the "Queen and the Craft," and that of "The M.W. the Grand Master" ; after which he should promptly give the brethren permission to smoke. It is generally understood that a cigarette with the "Sorbet" is part of the meal, and no disloyalty is indicated by this whiff or two prior to the Loyal Toast being given.

The Master is now working to his planned programme of speeches and music, but he should look at the visitor's book and request the D.C. to inform the brother proposing that toast which brethren are to be coupled with it, and also to advise those particular brethren that in due course they will be called upon to reply.

The Master must also keep a watchful eye upon the time, so that the toast of "Absent Brethren" may be given promptly at 9 o'clock. Some Lodges follow this toast with a special hymn. One which goes to the tune of "Eternal Father, strong to save," has as the first verse the following words :—

> "Great Architect of wond'rous power,
> Our brethren shield in danger's hour ;
> From rock and tempest, fire and foe,
> Protect them wheresoe'er they go.
> And evermore shall rise to Thee
> Our grateful thanks from land and sea."

4

MASONIC AFTER-DINNER SPEAKING

Faults to Avoid—What to Do—Mode of Delivery—Gaining and Holding Attention—Hints for a Master

WHEN we consider that after-dinner speaking is mainly a custom of the English-speaking people, it seems somewhat remarkable that good after-dinner speakers should be comparatively few and far between. It cannot be denied, however, that after-dinner speaking is an art which greatly adds to the social grace of a man, and the fact that Masonry calls for the exercise of this subtle art is another example of how the Craft helps to befit man for civil life.

Some consider after-dinner speaking to be a most difficult art to acquire, but it is not really so difficult as it seems to be at first thought, and probably the real reason underlying the poorness of after-dinner speeches is that sufficient time and thought are not given to the preparation of them. Curiously members of the Craft will devote hours to learning the ritual and rehearsing the ceremonies, but expect to be able to attain to an equal standard of success in the after-Lodge proceedings with practically no effort. It would be well if Lodges of Instruction gave attention to this matter by devoting say, ten minutes at the end of each meeting to impromptu speeches, and calling upon the younger members, thus giving them confidence before the time comes for them to reply to the "Officers" toast.

Curiously, also, everyone appreciates a good after-dinner speech and everyone knows what a bad speech is ; and almost every mason has experienced those pangs of agony when anticipating his turn to speak, and the equal, if not greater, distressful feelings when the effort has been made and failed in effect.

It is also equally curious that nine people out of ten fail to see why a speech has failed, and it may, therefore, be of some assistance if an attempt is made to analyse some of the principal reasons for failure.

The first has already been given, *viz.*, lack of preparation, which, of course, leads to illogical sequence of remarks, or absence of items of real interest. Another failing is to express too forcibly the inexperience of the speaker, which is probably only too obvious. Humour is a most difficult thing to introduce into a speech unless one is born with the gift of wit, and the story that does not "get across," as our American cousins say, is generally the one that has no bearing whatever upon the subject of the toast. Nothing upsets the inexperienced speaker more than telling a story that does not produce a smile. Then there is the person who lets his voice run away with him, and not being content with entertaining his hearers proceeds to bore them by keeping on too long. Some gabble and talk at such a rate that they are inaudible or, at least, most difficult to follow, whilst others seem to imagine that they are having a bed-time conversation with their wife, and must not talk above a whisper for fear they wake the baby.

Therefore, if you are going to make an after-dinner speech :—

1. Prepare it.
2. Rehearse it.
3. Time it.
4. Speak audibly.
5. Keep to your subject.
6. Be interesting.
7. End on a well-prepared phrase.

Hints on the preparation of a speech are given in another chapter. The rehearsal of a speech can be done by reading it aloud in a room and until proficiency is obtained ; by rehearsing it four or five times before delivery so that when the actual time comes for its delivery you will be well acquainted with it, and not liable to "er, er" in the middle, or be lost for an impressive conclusion.

The conclusion is often of greater import than the opening if a logical expression of thought has been followed, though a little stage management at the opening, such as pausing for silence, may be of advantage. Those who miss the opening remarks, through talking, will possibly go on talking later because they have lost the thread of your argument.

Style of delivery does, of course, count to a considerable extent, and it is probably true that orators are born and not made. Nevertheless, trial and practice results in considerable improvement.

Should you be Master or Master-elect, or replying upon any special occasion, e.g. after receipt of an honour or presentation, prepare yourself for the fact that rounds of applause will greet you on rising, and you will have to wait for them to die down before commencing your opening remarks. Steel yourself against being disturbed by this slight delay, which possibly seems like hours, though is probably not more than a minute.

Then, when delivering your speech, try not to fidget, i.e. avoid putting your hand in your pocket and then taking it out again ; do not finger a wine glass if you can resist the temptation, because you will try to look at it, and while doing so will be talking to the table top and not to the audience, and your voice may not carry.

If you have notes, get them ready in due time. Do not rise and say, "W.M. and brethren" and then go through your pockets trying to come across the missing piece of paper, meanwhile spluttering out stray remarks in an effort to hide your difficulty. No one will think you are feeling in your waistcoat pocket for a handkerchief. Notes need not be exhibited flamboyantly, but there is nothing to be ashamed of in having them, and it is a compliment to your audience that you have taken the trouble to previously think about what you are going to say.

To advise the after-dinner speaker to "speak up" is stating the obvious, but unfortunately this needs to be stressed. General faults are, (*a*) dropping the voice at the end of a sentence, (*b*) clipping the ends of words, and (*c*) speaking too quickly. The latter leads to the two former. From one hundred to one hundred and twenty words a minute is sufficiently fast. Experience in rate of speaking can be gained by reading from a marked paragraph of say two hundred and fifty words, out of a paper, against a watch.

Should you be speaking in a large room turn the head occasionally and slowly toward the left and right, while if you happen to be replying to a toast from a position where your back will be toward part of the audience, it is probably best to rise and face the chair, moving the head towards the majority of those present ; but do not try to turn right round during the speech.

Remember that only the most experienced speaker can successfully adopt the dramatic style. Generally it is better to adopt a conversational tone, using slight pauses and minor modulations of the voice to give emphasis, if such be needed, to certain sentences, and when the concluding phrase is reached to pause a moment, and adopt a slightly lower tone of voice.

Lastly, a few words of advice may be given to the new Master in the chair. His Installation Night is a heavy one ; in fact most of the nights of his year of office are. He will, therefore, be wise to deal abstemiously with the menu. Talking on an overloaded interior is not conducive to good after-dinner speaking, and some of the most eminent after-dinner speakers only partake of one or two courses, finding that by so doing their brains are kept more active. The Master may not have to deliver a long speech, like that of a Prime Minister at the Lord Mayor's Banquet, but he has several speeches to make and an important duty to perform in presiding over the proceedings. He will, therefore, be well advised to go slow with the "eats and the drinks."

It is often the one important year of a masonic lifetime and the avoidance of some little personal pleasure or delight to the palate is surely justifiable to ensure that both within and without the Lodge the year shall be a successful one.

By due preparation on his own part, by careful choice of speakers, and when needed the correct type of music, the Master can so plan the after-Lodge proceedings that everyone goes home feeling that it was a record meeting, a success which, if continued, leads to the impression of a memorable year.

On the other hand, the Master who gives the matter but little consideration on the grounds that he is not, and never will be an after-dinner speaker, is, it is to be feared, often only making a lazy man's excuse. Perhaps the effort has not been made, before taking the chair, to gain further proficiency in the gentle art. He relies on the speeches of others to make up for his own deficiency, and if there be many Past Masters in the Lodge who follow a similar course, their efforts probably may not materially improve the standard. The sacrifice of a little time, the putting forward of a little effort will produce a great difference, and vitally increase both the profit and the pleasure arising from the time spent at the festive board. His year of office in the chair provides a Master with a most valuable opportunity of expressing his own personality at the after-Lodge proceedings, and of adding to the tone of the gathering and with it to the reputation of the Lodge.

5

HINTS ABOUT DELIVERY OF SPEECHES

THE manner in which the Speeches are delivered is an important consideration. The following hints should be carefully noted, and acted on as far as possible, or needful, by any particular Brother :—

Stand up easily, without stiff posture, and face the whole or larger part of your audience. Do not play with objects on the table, or fidget about.

Speak clearly and with some amount of emphasis and expression, as the words or phrases demand. Do not hurry your discourse, pause at proper places, and, above all, do not drag out your remarks or become tedious.

Keep to your subject and do not digress from it to tell stories or make jokes. These are usually out of place, and should properly be left to a humorous entertainer. There is no Masonic obligation or duty to relate such things.

Add brightness to your manner, and if the occasion justifies, include some really witty remarks. Unless you are a practised speaker, however, this is dangerous, and may easily nullify the value of your speech.

Remember you have to be heard at the farthest point of the room, and not merely by those Brethren just around you. Hence your intonation and articulation should be clear and definite, every syllable being complete, words fully expressed and not slurred over.

A few hints may be given on general lines for business speeches :—

Address your remarks to the W.M., even in cases where you are dealing with the remarks of a previous speaker, but speak to the Lodge.

Take care to keep your voice at an easy pitch, and to vary or modulate it according to the nature or point of your remarks.

Keep your temper, and let your remarks be of a friendly or even conciliatory character, although you may be destroying the argument of an opponent.

If your case will be helped by an appearance of anger, let it be simulated and not real, or too prolonged. Raising trifling questions, or talking at large and at random, only bore or irritate those listening, but in general your audience become inattentive and irritated and less likely to listen to you another time.

When "other business" is permitted, avoid springing questions and matters which would be best dealt with privately in consultation with the W.M., the Treasurer, or Secretary. For instance, it is annoying to hear a member get up and complain (for the first time) of your Lodge summons being received in an unstamped envelope ; it is more fraternal to assume that Bro. Secretary did not omit the stamp on purpose, but may have been pressed with affairs and missed it.

If you are called to order, or some point is taken against you, or interruption by interjection, acquiesce in the decision, or suggestion from the W.M., or treat the interruption in a friendly spirit.

Be fluent, and alert, to meet any situation which may arise —preserve geniality and good temper, and sit down directly you have concluded, without saying, "I think that is all I have to say," or "I don't know that I can say anything more." If that is so, the best way of making the fact apparent is to sit down. Also, if you are unused to public speaking, there is no need to say so !

Watch your audience, and appreciate the effect of your speech upon them. If they are attentive and quiet, you are doing well ; if listless, gossipy, and given to toying with articles on the table, you are not. In the latter case, pull yourself together, make yourself more attractive in words, or gestures, and if no other course is successful, bring your remarks to a close.

Prepare your speech beforehand, and group speeches or phrases from the examples given, if such examples are not sufficiently apt for the occasion. Do not hesitate or drawl ; "er—er" is a sign of hesitation.

If you are not certain of your powers, study a little. Oratory and Elocution are largely matters of study and practice. Read books on the subject.

If you want to do well, you have to qualify yourself for the task.

The following hints will, however, help you to use or adapt the set speeches in this book to the best advantage.

Expression and Emphasis are needed. These can only be acquired in the first place by the use of the knowledge you have gained by study, and in the next place by careful attention and practice ; without which the diction, pronunciation and virility of your effort will fail, for the result will be cold, passionless and ineffective.

Gesture in ordinary speeches may be, and in many cases is, exceedingly useful, but there are parts where the effect of the sentences or addresses will be largely more apparent by a slight gesture of the hand, remembering to do so with the fingers open, but not with the hand clenched as if you wanted to drive home your words by punching or hitting someone or something.

Attitude goes for a great deal, and a careless position has a disturbing effect on the hearers, but an easy, graceful posture, leaning forward at times, and slight gestures of the hand at others, and by a sympathetic voice, you can be most effective, even if you are skilful already. Practice before a glass and see how you really do look.

Audibility and clearness of utterance are two most important points. Some rooms are well proportioned as to height and length, and possess acoustic properties of a high order ; others are not so, but are long and low, or have obstructive projections and decorations or chandeliers and so forth, all of which militate against the voice being heard at the other end of the room. Notice these things before you begin, but especially if the room is strange to you. Remember that a loud, shouting style is not needed, neither is a conversational tone given with the head down. Remember to direct your voice to someone at the end of the room. Clearness of utterance, the finishing of your words, not cutting or clipping the ends off, and a delivery which does not, by being too fast, make your words trip over each other—will all be found material in the effect to be produced. Allied to these is the phrasing, or division of sentences. One can often tell the effect of the effort to memorise by the jerky way in which the words are delivered. Where you have printed matter available, observe the punctuation ; where not, then in effect mentally punctuate your sentences so as to produce those intervals which will add to the emphasis or force of the words, as well as to give you the opportunity of taking breath. I am sure that, with care, concentration and assiduity, much can be done.

Method. For any additions to the set speeches which follow, you should be particular in arranging thought and speech on definite, well-ordered lines, for which a good cultivated memory will be found useful. This would give the power of utilising quotations and poetical excerpts in aid of the points being made by the speaker, and produce a variety in style and attractiveness. Style is very important as helping to make your speech into an interesting and helpful one.

Preparation. Under this head may fairly be put the practice of making short notes, or outlines, for additions to a speech, which, if need be, can include several lines of argument or ways of dealing with a subject, so that if some other speaker has hit upon some of your points, you will still be able to do creditably. Notes should be a guide only, not slavishly followed in altered circumstances, and the actual words to be used should not be memorised, but should be derived from the headings or notes. No one should attempt to make even a speech without preparation and thought. You might even go to the length of writing out a speech, and rehearsing it more than once, but on actual delivery discarding the written matter. If called on for a speech at short or a moment's notice, one has to exercise a good deal of concentrated thinking before speaking extemporaneously, for which purpose it is well to have acquired some of the qualities and powers I have indicated.

Elocution. Any speaker who has acquired the power of speaking well must also have some knowledge of the power of properly using and controlling the voice, but as an aid to expression that power can, to a large extent, be acquired by practice, and, believe me, it is well worth alike the attempt and some achievement.

General Points. Avoid a drawling or hesitating method of speaking. Pay attention to really good speakers, and note for practice the good points of manner, method and delivery. Compare such with your own powers and see where to amend them.

Do not make a long speech when your points can be made or sustained by a short, direct and clear one. Avoid repetition—if you have made yourself and your meaning clear, it is unnecessary.

Do not indulge in sarcasm ; it is too often misunderstood.

Talking at large or at random only bores or irritates those listening, and in general your audience becomes inattentive and less likely to listen to you another time.

Stand up with confidence, speak with sincerity and close with an effective period, and sit down without hesitation.

Modes of Address.   Be careful of these.   A bad start is often likely to produce a poor impression on the minds of your hearers, however good the main speech may be.   Some information under this head is given in later pages.

PROPOSING A TOAST

There is a growing custom for the W.M. to delegate a P.M. or other Brother to propose a toast, and this is a practice that affords some relief to the W.M. and also adds to the variety of the speeches.   Any Brother so called upon should, however, look upon it as a distinct honour and a privilege of distinction.

In all such cases the W.M. hands the gavel to the proposer, who, for the time being, wields the authority and power of the W.M. and leads the fire, and also calls on those who have to respond.

The art of after-dinner speaking should be diligently cultivated, as it is always a pleasure to listen to an able and fluent speaker.

RESPONDING TO A TOAST

Admittedly, replying to a toast is sometimes more difficult than proposing one, because unfortunately in many instances the courtesy of a warning a day or two before will not have been extended to you.   One therefore has to be on the alert all the time the proposer of the toast is talking, ready to note and seize upon any point or points which will be of value in connection with one's reply. If he is a poor speaker, it is quite probable that there will not be any outstanding points to take advantage of, and you will have to fall back upon your own knowledge and skill entirely to do justice to the occasion.

If you have nothing of moment to say do not disguise the fact by becoming unduly complimentary. It is rather futile, for example, for a very young M.M. in responding for the visitors to say, "the working was the finest he had ever seen." It would probably be better to content oneself with quite a modest effort, saying :—

"It has given me great pleasure to be present to-night, and to share with the other visiting brethren your excellent hospitality for which you have undoubtedly merited our thanks. This is a short speech, but not the shortest, which, I believe, is 'Guilty.' That word is both my plea and my excuse, for being young in the Craft I am not experienced in replying to this toast."

As a visitor to a Lodge it is generally considered proper to express some words of appreciation to the immediate host and to the W.M. and the Lodge as a whole. Platitudes should be avoided and every effort made to say something original. Those with gifts in that direction may have recourse to the relation of appropriate humorous anecdotes, or give a description of an interesting Masonic custom or other item of general interest. Very often it is possible to gain inspiration from the Lodge banner or jewel, or from the name or some peculiarity of the Lodge, and to use this as the text.

The correct method of address is to begin by addressing the W.M., and if Grand Officers are present to say, Worshipful Master, Grand Officers and Brethren. Speak quietly but clearly, use simple direct language, think out the outlines of what has to be said, and say everything in sequence, gradually building up the purport of the remarks to a logical or natural conclusion.

Any reference to personal rank or attainments should be avoided or dealt with very modestly, as, after all is said and done, all present are Brothers, all meet on the level, and all ultimately attain the same state.   All earthly honours are fleeting and the wisest of Masons know not the day or hour when the Great Tyler shall summon one and all to the same common end.

6

PREPARING AFTER-DINNER SPEECHES

GENERALLY speaking every member of the Craft knows that at some time or other he will be called upon for a speech. Even if he be one of those who do not aspire to office, it is probable that sooner or later he will be called upon to reply for the visiting brethren. The Freemason who does travel the road of office toward the Master's chair realises that he will, from time to time, be called upon to speak and that, when he becomes Master of the Lodge, quite an amount of after-dinner speaking will form part of his duties whilst he holds that high office. Therefore, just as it is advisable to begin to learn the ritual at an early stage in one's Masonic career, so is it also advisable to devote some attention to the social side by preparing the foundation for after-dinner speaking. Practice makes perfect, but if really instructive worthwhile speeches are to be made, then reading and preparation are essential as well as practice in delivery.

The first stage is probably that of observation, of listening carefully to other speakers, and making brief notes of interesting points. The second stage is reading and noting as one reads. There are many books published which contain much matter of interest that could be introduced into after-dinner speeches with profit and pleasure to the brethren, and if, when the book is read, a note of suitable paragraphs is made on the flyleaf or in a small note book, quick reference can be made when the occasion arises calling for the preparation of a speech.

For example, in the little volume, "Five Minute Talks on Freemasonry," by W. Bro. S. M. Hills, the following paragraph appears :—

"To-day, there are two Deacons, but in England, previous to the Union of 1813, Deacons were not generally recognised by the 'Moderns,' though they were appointed by the 'Antients'. They serve as assistants to the Master, and the Senior Warden. The title of their office is derived from the Greek 'Diakonos' meaning a servant in a position of trust. As the Junior Deacon acts as the servant or messenger of the Senior Warden, so in addition to the responsibility of admitting candidates on proof does the Inner Guard act as the servant or messenger of the Junior Warden, he providing the means of authority by which the Outer Guard or Tyler can permit candidates or visitors to pass him and enter the Lodge."

Mark this paragraph and then, on the flyleaf of the book put "Officers' Toast," or in a notebook under the heading "Officers' Toast" put " 'Five Minute Talks on Freemasonry' —Hills." Then when a speech for the Officers' Toast has to be prepared, the notebook supplies the guide to a possible idea, and by using the above paragraphs as an inspiration one might proceed as follows :—

(1) The officers of a Lodge afford a useful lesson of the value and importance of the team spirit in Freemasonry.

(2) However able the Master may be in the discharge of the duties annexed to his important office, the efficient performance of our beautiful and impressive ceremonies must largely depend on the officers, and in appointing his officers the Master places his trust in them, that they will loyally co-operate with him to to the fullest possible extent and that the reputation of the Lodge may be maintained during his year in the chair.

(3) In this connection it is perhaps of some interest to observe that the word "Deacon" is derived from the Greek "Diakonos"—meaning a servant in a position of trust.

(4) The Senior Deacon acts as a trusted servant and messenger of the Master, and the Junior Deacon fulfils the same duties for the Senior Warden, while the Inner Guard also acts as a trusted messenger for the Junior Warden by providing authority for the Outer Guard to permit candidates or visitors to pass him and enter the Lodge.

(5) In like manner the brethren place their trust in the Treasurer when they elect him, and the Master in the Secretary, and the D.C. when he appoints them.

(6) The dictionary gives as one meaning of the word "Trust"—"Firm conviction in another's realibility." From what we have seen in the past, and what we know personally concerning the characters of our officers, I feel sure that the trust which the Master has reposed in them will not prove to be misplaced. I therefore ask you to rise and drink the health of the officers of the Lodge.

(7) Coupling with it the name of Bro. . . . . , Senior Deacon.

From this outline speech it will be seen that from one paragraph in a book it is possible to build up quite an interesting little effort somewhat different from the ordinary, thus helping to command the attention of those who listen.

One can do the same thing with stories by exercising a little ingenuity. The following is taken from a cutting from the *Glasgow Herald*, which described an alleged visit of Mr. Ramsay MacDonald to a mental hospital where he was introduced to a convalescent patient as the Prime Minister, when the patient said, "They'll soon cure you of that here. I know, because when I came in I was Earl Haig." A Master responding to the toast of his health could quite well tell this story, and go on to say, "When I was installed Master of this Lodge I possibly felt to too great a degree my own importance, but the Past Masters soon cured me of that."

By that means, a story having no relation to the toast is given one, and becomes appropriate.

Admittedly, it is not easy to find just the ideas or stories one wants at any given moment unless a systematic method of building up reference matter is employed. A scrap book or commonplace book, coupled with a notebook, is therefore, of considerable value. By subscribing to a Masonic journal, and noting from speeches or articles published therein suitable paragraphs and recording the reference in a note-book, or extracting and entering the paragraph in the commonplace book, the beginner will, at the sacrifice of a few minutes a week, quickly build up a system of reference which will prove invaluable as the years pass by.

As has been stated in a previous chapter, the beginner will probably be wise in writing out his speech, and in reading it over aloud a few times before he has to deliver it, but in addition notes will probably be of advantage. These can take the form of main headings typed, or boldly written on a small piece of card so that they can be read quickly. A post card serves very well for this purpose. Thus, reverting to the speech concerning "The Officers," the following notes would serve as an aid to the memory, should nervousness intervene :—

(1) Lesson of value of trust.

(2) Master must rely on officers—Co-operation essential.

(3) Deacon—Greek—Diakonos—Servant of Trust.

(4) Master's servant—S.D.
    S.W.'s   servant—J.D.
    J.W.'s   servant—I.G.

(5) Treas.—Sec.—D.C.

(6) Dictionary—Trust—"Firm conviction in another's reliability."

(7) Coupled—Bro. . . . .—S.D.

The numbers given above correspond with the numbers placed against the various paragraphs in the outline speech.

With notes such as these to guide him the speaker is unlikely to overlook a point, and thus spoil the logical sequence of his talk, yet they are sufficiently condensed to be clear when written on a post card, which in turn is of suitable size for carrying in the pocket, yet not obtrusive at the dinner table.

Reading books concerning the Craft undoubtedly provides an aid to the production of speeches, and small doses of instruction can be given to the brethren present in an entertaining manner by this means ; but one can also bring in points from the ritual which add interest.   Thus in dealing with the subject of benevolence, a Master might point out that *the wisest of us knows not how soon* fortunes or circumstances may change.   While Masonry is not a mutual benefit society, it is of interest to remember that the seventh regulation of Anderson's Constitutions of 1723 provided that "Every new Brother at his making is to deposit something for the Relief of the indigent and decay'd Brethren," whilst Anthony Sayer, the first Grand Master, presented a petition to the Quarterly Communication of Grand Lodge on 21st November, 1724, for relief, only seven years after his election to the head of the Craft.

One is not necessarily confined, however, to Craft reading. Use can often be made of the contents of other books, and of the contents of daily papers.   Poetry can sometimes be introduced with effect.   Thus, again, when dealing with the subject of benevolence, the words of Alexander Pope apply :—

"In Faith and Hope the world will disagree,
But all mankind's concern is charity."

The following short poem by Gretta Woodbridge would form a fitting conclusion to the toast of the "Initiate" or that of the newly installed Master :—

"Isn't it strange that princes and kings
And clowns that caper in sawdust rings,
And ordinary folk like you and me
Are builders of Eternity ?

To each is given a bag of tools,
An hour glass and a book of rules,
And each must build, ere his hour is flown,
A stumbling-block or a stepping-stone."

Reference has previously been made to Kipling's poems ; his prose is also useful. For instance, the story of "Kim" provides a most impressive lesson on the value that can be set upon a Masonic apron and a Grand Lodge certificate which could be brought into a speech in shortened and paraphrased form thus :—

You have all at least heard of, if not read, Kipling's poems and prose. His story of Kim is of distinct Masonic interest. It relates the experiences of a child, left motherless, whose father became a drunkard, loafing through India with his three-year-old baby, till he came into contact with a woman who took opium, and he died as white men do who take to drink and drugs beneath India's scorching sun. Before he passed over he dwelt upon those things that would eventually make little Kim a man. They were Kim's birth certificate (which would prove him white), a Lodge clearance certificate, and a Masonic certificate. Eventually the discovery of these led to Kim being properly educated and he did well. The lesson we learn from this is the faith exemplified in the Craft, that undying faith which our less fortunate brethren place in their comrades, and we realise that while some fall by the wayside owing to their own failings, the great majority do so on account of unforeseen calamity. Can we, in fact, dare we risk breaking faith with those who have passed to G.L. above, and who in passing relied upon us to fulfil the tenets of the Craft. The call has never been greater than it is to-day, and I ask you, therefore, to give as liberally as you can, but with fairness to those near to you, not for the hope of reward but for the pleasure of giving.

Almost everyone has a copy of Tennyson's poems in the house, and the following extract, in which that poet virtually portrays Freemasonry in a few lines would form an impressive ending to the toast of the "Initiate" by explaining that they were the vows of a young knight, who, placing his hand on the sword of King Arthur, swore :—

> "To reverence his conscience as his King.
> To break the heathen and uphold the Christ.
> To ride abroad redressing human wrongs.
> To speak no slander, no, nor listen to it.
> To honour his own words as if his God's.
> To lead sweet lives in purest chastity.
> To love one maiden only, cleave to her.
> To worship her by years of noble deeds.
> Not only to keep down the base in man,
> But to teach him high thought and amiable words,
> And courtliness and the desire of fame,
> And love of truth and all that makes a man."

It may be said in passing that, naturally, to be most effective, poetic quotations should be learned by heart, or at least read beforehand many times so that if they are read, they can be read with knowledge and full feeling.

This chapter may now be brought to a conclusion by examples in the use of the daily paper or magazine as a source of inspiration. The following is a cutting from *The Times*, part of which would fit well into the speech of an Immediate Past Master :—

(1) "Human life is one long procession of goals reached and passed ; of objects sought and attained, relinquished, or forgotten, but anyway removed from the field of sight to give place to others. Sometimes that to which we look forward is so compelling in its attractiveness that it seems to blot out all beside. Nothing else can live in the range of foresight. We must have that one thing or perish. But it is not

always so in this imperfect world. The forward look is often monopolised by dark foreboding or sheer dread.

(2) "It is only in the cold light of retrospect that we see how slight a thing could once fill our whole horizon with desire or fear, how small an angle it subtended in the general scheme. The real crisis of the look ahead comes to those who have had most practice in it.

(3) "The man who, through gathering years of failing health, becomes conscious of his uncertain hold on life, sees his ultimate outlook bounded by a blind barrier earth-wide and heaven-wide. There is no way through, round or over. Knowledge and experience are dumb before it. But, though science, skill, and subtlety are of no avail, man is not yet at the end of his resources. It helps him to remember how often before fresh beauty and new objects of aspiration have revealed themselves just when he felt that he had come to the limit of possibility. His spirit still finds itself impelled to believe and to act on the belief, that even beyond the veil which is drawn across his mortal span there lies a continuing field of endeavour and achievement."

The speech could open with the first paragraph (1), closing with the word foresight. Then go on to explain how, since the day of initiation one had looked forward to gaining the chair of one's Mother Lodge. Next, applying paragraph (2), one could go on to say, "In the light of cold retrospect one is conscious of many omissions and many failings, which had occurred in a year of office, that to the occupant appeared to be all too short for the full attainment of one's ambition." Follow with paragraph (3), and add, "The man who, through gathering years of failing health" ... etc. .... (to the end of the quotation). The closing words might be something like this: "However, the Master just out of the chair realises to the full the help he has received from others, from the officers, and from the past Masters, and sees a vision of continued useful Masonic life in the work he can do toward advancing the interests of the Craft as a whole, and the Lodge in particular by imparting knowledge and rendering assistance to all who come within his sphere of activity."

Again, there appeared in the *Sunday Express* an article entitled "The Men Who Rule the Empire," from which the following paragraphs are taken :—

"The man in the street knows little of the personalities or the powers of the patient servants of the Crown who are the real administrators of the Empire . . ."

"One day a book may be written based on the archives of the Crown Agents' office and the Colonial Office—a book on the romance of individual achievement and of the courage and self-possession of unassuming men . . ."

"They are masters of the infinitesimal, these minor kings, shrewd appraisers of the important.

"While knowing the significance of the five-hundred-year-old tortoise which frisks in the palace gardens of the Queen of the Tonga Islands, they also are intimately versed in the psychology of the wild tribes on the upper reaches of the Fly River.

"To you and me these matters seem unimportant. Actually it is a knowledge of trifles which keeps peace in the world. The Indian Mutiny was started by cartridge oil . . ."

"There are other men, however, outside the Colonial service, who have earned the gratitude which they will never wholly receive, for the Empire as a whole knows, through their own modesty, so little of them . . ."

"And there are others who are distinguished by the length of service they have rendered."

This can quite readily be applied as a speech for the toast of the "Past Masters of the Lodge." The beginning is probably quite obvious :—

"The Young Master Mason or junior member of the Lodge possibly knows little or nothing concerning the patient work of those who have attained the highest honour the Lodge can bestow, and who are now numbered among the rulers in the Craft and Past Masters of the Lodge. One day a Lodge history may be written in which some painstaking author will at least faithfully describe their virtues, if with mercy he overlooks their failings. A writer once described the Colonial Civil Servants as being 'Masters of the infinitesimal, minor kings, shrewd appraisers of the important,' and went on to say 'while knowing the significance of the five-hundred-year-old tortoise which frisks in the palace gardens of the Queen of the Tonga Islands, they are also intimately versed in the psychology of the wild tribes on the upper reaches of the Fly River.' Our P.M.'s may know nothing concerning the Queen of Tonga or the tribes on the Fly River, but their years of service and experience has placed them in the happy position of being able to give sound advice both to the Master and the Lodge. Some are distinguished for having an evergreen knowledge of the ritual, others for length of service, while our oldest P.M. W. Bro. ——— can always be relied upon to be able to say what it was exactly that the Lodge did in eighteen-eighty something."

Enough has probably been said to indicate means by which the novice can gain assistance in building up speeches, and at the same time give them an original aspect. They will still be to a large degree his own, for be it remembered that he will have selected the cuttings or reference matter, and he will have applied them to illustrate or emphasise the points in his speech, thus presenting in the speech his own personality or view-point, though he has profited from the effort of others to obtain a start. Of course, as time goes by and greater confidence and experience is gained, the speaker will find himself able to build up speeches on his own account and particularly if he follows the advice given and reads he will find that ideas come to him quite readily. This is a feature he will find invaluable when unexpectedly called upon to reply to a speech, which subject is dealt with in a later chapter.

Finally, if you are going to propose a toast for the first time, take a little trouble to make sure beforehand that you can do the "Fire" correctly by practising it at home in company with a Masonic friend, or alternatively ask the Preceptor of the L. of I. to go through it with you. It is one of those little things that look very simple, but are not so simple as they look when you take the lead for the first time ; and because it is a really old-time custom it is worth doing well.

7

GRAND OFFICERS AND PROVINCIAL GRAND OFFICERS

ENOUGH has probably been said in the previous chapters to indicate that real proficiency in after-dinner speaking can only be acquired by means of constant practice coupled with careful thought and extensive reading. Everyone, however, has to make a start, and whilst it is not suggested that the following speeches should be learned by heart and repeated in parrot-like fashion, it is hoped that they will provide some indication for the beginner concerning how he could or should proceed. Circumstances alter cases, and possibly only parts of an outline speech given may be of service, or it may well happen that parts of more than one of the outline speeches may be welded together in compiling a speech, or in providing a beginning or ending. The reader must to a degree exercise his own thought in the matter. It cannot be denied, however, that many a newly-installed Master fails to realise the important trust imposed upon him in connection with the after-Lodge proceedings.

It has already been pointed out that the first duty which befalls the Master after dinner is to say Grace (unless the brethren sing it) and after that to propose the toasts of "The Queen and the Craft," and "The M.W. the Grand Master." Nothing need be, and generally, nothing should be said in proposing these toasts. Should the Queen or the Grand Master have recently suffered an illness, or the latter have performed some action of very particular Masonic moment, then perhaps a few appropriate words might be said concerning the matter, but not otherwise. Neither is any reply given to these toasts.

In proposing the toast of the "Grand Officers" discretion can also be exercised. One need say but very little if there is no Grand Lodge Officer present to reply, yet the toast should always be honoured. It must be remembered that the number of appointments to Grand Rank each year are comparatively few, and it is a distinct honour to have obtained one. In the main the Grand Officers represent a body of men who have voluntarily given their brains and service to the Craft for a number of years, a remark which also applies to Provincial Grand Lodge officers and to Brethren of London Grand Rank. Of the latter, most Lodges have at least one or more representatives present at each meeting, and therefore there is someone to reply to the toast.

In proposing the toast of "Provincial Grand Lodge Officers" or that of "London Grand Rank," one should always bear in mind that the change from wearing a light to a dark blue collar was an honour merited by service. Whatever is said concerning other toasts, dignity should be the keynote, and due reference should be made concerning the services of an individual of high rank to the Lodge, if, of course, the remark applies. Where a number of such brethren belong to the Lodge it is probably wise to vary the brother replying, so that each is called upon in turn, thus maintaining the interest, both of the person coupled with the toast and of the brethren in general.

It has to be remembered that there are limitations to what one can say in reply to a set toast, and adherence to the practice of always coupling the name of the senior Grand or Provincial Grand Officer with the toast places an undue tax upon the ingenuity of that speaker, practised hand though he may be.

GRAND OFFICERS PRESENT AND PAST

General Ideas

Honour is mark of merit for long and distinguished service—Appointment of Grand Officers dates back over

200 years—Respected for personality—Appreciated for faithful discharge of duties—Set example of integrity and honour for others to follow—Sacrifice of leisure time for the benefit of the brethren.

(1)   TOAST OF THE GRAND OFFICERS, PRESENT
AND PAST

"Truly the sun never sets on Freemasonry; its working is going on all the time both within and without our many Lodges. When we are in bed others in different parts of the world are performing ceremonies, and the Lodges which owe adherence to the Grand Lodge of England are spread over all four quarters of the globe. Whilst the great work of keeping the organisation together as one piece of smoothly working machinery is to an extent due to the continued efforts of the Grand Secretary and his staff, it must not be overlooked that a vast amount of voluntary work is done by the President of the Board of General Purposes, the President of the Board of Benevolence, Provincial and District Grand Masters, and Grand Secretaries, together with the efforts of many distinguished brethren who devote much time to presiding over the destinies of Lodges of Instruction, Benevolent Associations and other organisations connected with the Craft. These are the brethren who by their indefatigable interest and work for Freemasonry have earned the honours which the M.W. the Grand Master has bestowed upon them, and it is not only right that we should honour them by drinking this toast when we meet together, but a pleasure, because it enables us to express our indebtedness to them. This evening we are honoured by the presence of W. Bro. —— who as most of you know has ——, etc. We welcome him as a worthy representative of a body of men who reflect honour upon the Craft, and I couple his name with this toast."

(2)   TOAST OF THE GRAND OFFICERS [1]

"Brethren, I ask you to honour this important toast as a symbol of our loyalty to those brethren to whom the M.W. the Grand Master has given honour and rank to help him in the well ruling and governing of the Craft. We appreciate the work that they have done, and the sacrifice of leisure time they made on our behalf in discharging their duties, and are glad to welcome them among us as distinguished brethren, whose presence inspires us to still greater effort."

(3)   TOAST OF THE GRAND OFFICERS [2]

"Some may hold the opinion that Grand Rank marks the summit of attainment in a Masonic career, for which there is much substantive argument, but I should not like the brethren of this Lodge to be under the mistaken idea that the task of working for the Craft is finished with the attainment of that high rank. Those who wear the Grand Lodge Clothing are those who have worked and are continuing to work day by day for the benefit of the Craft as a whole. Perhaps I can well call to your mind what Grand Rank implies by quoting the following words of the late Pro. Grand Master, Lord Ampthill, uttered at a meeting of the United Grand Lodge of England on the occasion of the Grand Festival on April 27th, 1932. In addressing the new Grand Officers he said, 'Each and everyone of you has a definite and constant duty, and that duty is to maintain the honour and dignity of your rank, to prove to the world by virtuous, amiable and discreet conduct that Freemasonry is neither a convivial association nor a mere benefit society. The badges with which you will be invested are meant to not only point out your superior rank, but also to remind you that it is your particular duty to afford assistance and instruction to all those below you.' Those last words are, it may be said, an exact definition of the work those officers do perform and have performed for many years. We find them still working as Secretaries and Treasurers of our Lodges, as Preceptors of Lodges of Instruction, as Presidents of Benevolent Associations, always ready and always willing to find time to do something more for the good of the Craft as a whole. It is therefore a pleasure to comply with our duty by honouring this toast with all sincerity."

It would be presumptuous to indicate forms of reply by Grand Lodge officers, but perhaps the following words expressed by Lord Ampthill in 1932 may be printed here :

"I hope that you, Brethren, who are about to be invested this evening, will allow me to offer you a little piece of advice. Please try to break away from a deplorable convention which has too often come to my notice. When you are called upon to respond for the Grand Officers, beware of saying that you do not know what are your duties as such. Those conventional utterances are, to say the least of it, not complimentary to the Grand Master or conducive to the dignity of your rank. Modesty, of course, is becoming, but there is nothing to commend in false modesty which is, indeed, the pride that apes humility."

Similar remarks, one feels, might be applied in connection with the replies one hears to the toast of "Provincial Grand Officers" and the toast of London Grand Rank.

PROVINCIAL GRAND OFFICERS

General Ideas.

Honour a mark of merit—Assist Prov. Grand Master in Administration of the Province—Work done for brethren and Lodges—Set example of adherence to tenets of the Craft—Overseers or Prefects to guide and assist others in the work.

(4) TOAST OF PROVINCIAL GRAND LODGE OFFICERS

"Masonry being a progressive science, many pass from being raised to the sublime degree of an M.M. through the various offices until they attain the highest honour the Lodge can bestow by being elected to, and installed in the Chair of K.S. In due course they become P.M.'s, but their work is not finished. As guides and counsellors they form the backbone of the Lodge, and perhaps the Provincial Grand Master may honour them by investing them with the collar and jewel of a Provincial Grand Officer. Our Craft quickly grew to dimensions which necessitated the subdivision of authority, and some years before the Union of the Antients and the Moderns, Provincial Grand Officers were appointed. In course of time the list of officers became extended to that which we know to-day, and our officers of Provincial Rank are the Overseers or Prefects to whom the Provincial Grand Master looks to assist him in governing his Province. We have been fortunate in this Lodge to have been honoured by the appointment of Bros. —— to Provincial Rank, while also with us to-night are Bros. —— as visitors. We honour this toast with pleasure, and express our sincere appreciation of the work these brethren do for the benefit of the Craft as a whole, and this Province of —— in particular."

8

WELCOME TO VISITORS

It is suggested that welcome to visitors should be given in Lodge during a convenient interval. It is futile to offer a "hearty welcome" in terms at the fag-end of the evening, when the visit is practically concluded and many Brethren, and even visitors, have had to leave.

(5)   TO VISITORS OF SPECIAL EMINENCE

(*Addressing them*) : "Brethren, On behalf of this Lodge and its members, it gives me special pleasure to offer you our fraternal greetings, and to cordially welcome you amongst us. We regard it as a singular honour that you should be present this evening. We trust your visit will be agreeable and interesting to you, as we are certain it is and will be to ourselves. We look forward, as a result, to increased activity and a greater exercise of the principles and tenets of the Craft by all our members."

(Here might be given some indication of the reason for the special visit, the connection of any of the visitors with the Lodge, and unless previously or subsequently announced, some particulars of the rank and services of the visitors.)

"In thus bidding you welcome, we desire to express our appreciation and recognition of the great services you have rendered to the Craft and to assure you we shall look back to the proceedings this evening and your participation in them with special pleasure and satisfaction.

Brethren of the ———— Lodge ! I call on you to show your concurrence with my remarks, and to do fitting honour to our distinguished Brethren, by being upstanding, and saluting them with, etc."

(6) *Reply*.

In ordinary cases, it would be sufficient to expand the usual formula thus :—

"W.M. and Brethren, We thank you for your fraternal welcome and salutation, and greet you well."

On special occasions the senior Grand Officer present might with advantage previously make some remarks on the occasion.

(7)   A Shorter Form of Welcome to
    Grand Officers

"Brethren, On your behalf, as well as my own, it is now my duty, as it is my pleasure and privilege, to welcome (names and rank of visitors) to our Lodge this evening. I am quite confident you will respond in that fraternal and affectionate manner which will indicate to our visitors how much we appreciate the honour they have conferred upon us by their presence. To order, Brethren, and salute, etc., etc. (if appropriate)."

(8) *Reply*.

By Grand Officers, by their senior, the usual formula will suffice for all the visitors included. If, however, Brethren of other ranks only are present, one should formally reply :—
" W.M. and Brethren, we thank you."

To Visiting Brethren from Overseas

In most Overseas Jurisdictions more formality is observed in the reception and welcome of visitors of any rank from the Homeland and elsewhere than is generally done here. Hence it is very desirable that special attention should be taken here.

(9) "Brethren, We are, as you will have observed, honoured by the presence of visitors from Overseas, being members of our own or other Jurisdictions. In your name, I offer them, individually and collectively, our most cordial and fraternal greetings and welcome."

(The D.C. might here announce the name, rank, Lodge and Jurisdiction of each Brother, who could at the same time be presented to the W.M.)

"Without in the least derogating from our general welcome, I should like to refer specially to Bro. ———— of ———— an Overseas Brother of our own Jurisdiction (or, as the case may be, of English or Colonial origin). His presence here is an assurance of loyalty to our Sovereign and Commonwealth, to our M.W.G.M., and of affection and zeal for the Craft. As regards Bro. ———— of ———— (and others of Jurisdictions at amity with our own), they come from Jurisdictions recognised by the U.G.L. of England, and we hope their presence will prove an indication of amity and unity in the Craft universal."

(Salute if appropriate.)

(10) *Reply*.

By a Brother, the senior in rank or selected previously by the W.M.

"W.M. and Brethren, We thank you for your fraternal welcome to your Lodge, an honour we highly appreciate, and our visit will be an outstanding memory and pleasure of our Masonic experience here."

(Or the reply may be quite formal.)

Visitors in Ordinary Cases

The usual visitors to a Lodge are often well known and attend with some frequency. Still there are others who are paying their first visit. Although less formality is needed, yet it would often be appropriate that more than a mere announcement at the portal should be adopted.

(11) ## TOAST TO THE VISITORS [1]

"Brethren, The presence here this evening of several visiting Brethren calls for an expression of our pleasure and welcome. We trust their visit will enable them to realise the value to us of their support, and the sincerity of our hope they will enjoy our company. On your behalf and my own, I greet the Brethren, and wish them well."

(The names, etc., might be given by the D.C. and salute if appropriate.)

(12) ## TOAST TO THE VISITORS [2]

"Brethren, we are honoured this evening by the presence of . . . brethren from other Lodges. Every year on Installation night, the Master and Wardens are reminded of the need for visiting, and in fact visiting is one of the oldest customs of our Order, dating back to the days of the Operative Lodges, when a travelling brother was given food, refreshment, and if need be a place to rest his body, before he set out again upon his travels. We naturally hope our visitors have been impressed by our ceremonies, and feel themselves refreshed by what has been provided after the Lodge has closed. Their presence has encouraged us and we thank them for sojourning among us. On behalf of the Master and Wardens I welcome them all, and by command of the Master, couple with this toast the names of Those . . ."

(13) *Reply*.

By one of the visitors for all :—

"W.M. and Brethren of the ———— Lodge, On behalf of the visiting Brethren, I offer your our grateful thanks."

HONORARY MEMBERS VISITING

Some honorary members attend with great regularity, and may be regarded as ordinary members, but it is well, when an honorary member attends but seldom, to make an appropriate reference to the visitor. Care should be taken in cases where the visitor is a Grand Officer. One (or part) of the forms of welcome already given, with a proper variation, or the following may be used.

(14) "Brethren, W. Bro. ———— (rank), who is with us this evening, is, as you know, one of the honorary members of the Lodge. He was one of the Consecrating Officers of the Lodge (or as the case may be). In consequence, we hold him in special regard and are particularly glad to see him here. On your behalf, I bid him welcome."

(Salute if appropriate.)

(15) JOINING MEMBER (*after election*)

"Brother ————. The Brethren have by their unanimous vote elected you a Joining Member of this Lodge. We welcome your accession to the Lodge, and from the known character of your Masonic work we look forward with confidence to the advantage of your assistance and ability in the conduct of the affairs and ceremonial of the Lodge. We extend to you the right hand of fellowship (does so) and you will now take your seat among your new Brethren and Fellows."

(16) *Reply*.

"W.M. and Brethren, I offer you my heartfelt thanks for the honour conferred upon me, and assure you that I will do all in my power to merit your confidence in me."

REPLYING FOR "THE VISITORS"

We have left behind with the Victorian era that happy practice whereby everyone present at a social evening helped to contribute toward the enjoyment of all by singing, playing or reciting, but though the practice of entertaining in our own homes may have decreased, one still expresses thanks for hospitality received. The practice of toasting the "Visiting Brethren" is a means whereby a general welcome can be extended, and a thanks returned, and it is to be hoped that this pleasing custom will never die out, at least so far as the Craft is concerned.

It cannot be denied but that the visitor owes some return to his personal host, and the Lodge, for the hospitality and instruction provided, and in replying for the visitors, while he will, naturally, open or close his speech by expressing his thanks, he can also contribute to the common pool of knowledge by saying something worth while. To be able to do so largely only calls for a little preparation and fore-thought. Fore-warned is fore-armed. If a Mason knows he is going to visit a Lodge, he knows that he *may* be called upon to reply for the visitors. Therefore, why not go prepared for the task ? If not called upon, the notes can remain undisturbed in one's pocket, but if called upon, and the proposer of the toast does not provide any points which can be quickly noted and dealt with in reply, then the originally prepared matter will prove to be a boon and a blessing. Practice makes perfect, and in judiciously collect-ing suitable material and welding it into a speech, many a member of the Craft can contribute his effort toward making the evening a success by suitably impressing the Brethren.

To the older member of the Craft, responding to the toast of "The Visitors" provides a valuable opportunity of making some return for the hospitality that has been enjoyed. The warning may be short, but nevertheless the thoughtful Mason will have gone prepared in case of need, and will have some ideas or an outline speech in mind, and will adapt it where necessary to meet the needs created by comments made by the brother who proposed the toast. It always seems to the author rather ungrateful when replying to a toast to open by saying that until that moment you had thoroughly enjoyed yourself, or alternatively that you were thoroughly enjoying the soup when Bro. D. C. advised you that you would have to reply for the visitors and that entirely spoiled the rest of the meal.

It may, generally speaking, be said to be unwise for a visitor to comment upon the form of ritual used in the Lodge. There are many rituals in use to-day, each of which has points of merit and claims to antiquity. It is invidious for a visitor to draw comparisons, though he might sometimes express interest in the differences he noted, provided he does not make any claim that the working of his own Lodge is superior. Rather than comment upon the wonderful working, which may not have been wonderful (and the intelligent members present know it) it is better to remark upon the sincere way in which the Master tried to impress the candidate. Phrases from the ritual can often be worked into a reply with good effect.

One might begin a reply for the visitors in the following manner :—

(17) "It is a pleasure to respond to the enthusiastic welcome which the proposer of this toast gave to the visitors. A welcome, which I might perhaps without presumption say, I expected because of the kindly way in which Bro. Tyler looked after me when I arrived this evening. His kindly attentions immediately made me feel at home. Having been taught to be cautious I do not propose to bite the daintily baited hook which the proposer presented in referring to the working within the Lodge, beyond saying that I, in common with the other visitors present, was greatly impressed with the sincerity with which the whole ceremony was carried out. Those who have taken an interest in the early days of the Craft and have read the story of the Lodge of Reconciliation, can appreciate how differences in working came about, but it is always of interest to visitors to note variations. I am glad to notice that you use the term Visitors (or Visiting Brethren) because to my mind that term has some Masonic significance. It comes from the French Visé, meaning 'vouched for,' and

every member of the Craft who visits a Lodge has to be vouched for. I would, therefore, in conclusion express my thanks to my personal host, Bro. ————, who vouched for me on this occasion, and to you brethren for the kindly way in which you have received and entertained me."

Here is another form of speech which may be found useful when called upon to reply for the visitors, being one which imparts some information concerning old-time customs.

(18) "Having thoroughly enjoyed your kindly welcome, your working, and your hospitality, for which I thank you, I do not wish to be considered ungrateful or lacking in interest in your proceedings, when I confess that at moments I found my mind wandering back over the days gone by. Visiting is a delight to the enthusiastic mason, it enables him to gain fresh viewpoints, and to those in office it is sometimes a pleasing change to be able to sit back and listen, free from responsibility. I almost regret that the old-time custom for a Mason to seek admission as a visitor has in these days of banquets tended to pass away. Looking through the histories of old Lodges one finds many curious things. One learns, for example, that the Tyler delivered summonses, drew the Lodge upon the floor, collected dues and also the visitors' fees. I did not have to pay the Tyler when I arrived. There was a period when the Strong Arm Lodge 45 (which commenced in 1733 and has celebrated its bi-centenary) paid tenpence for a Lodge supper, and threepence for beer, while the visitor paid half-a-crown, except when funds were very flush, and then everyone enjoyed a free meal and refreshment. I judge from what you have put before your guests to-night that it is no longer possible to cater at those prices. Again from the history of the Old Globe Lodge No. 22, in one set of bye-laws it was stated that 'The Master shall be acquainted by the S.W. when it is 10 o'clock when he shall immediately close the

Lodge, or sooner, if business permits . . . Any person remaining in the house after 11 o'clock to forfeit the sum of one shilling.' There are other speeches to be made, and other items to be enjoyed, so as the hour is getting late, I will not place others or myself under the risk of being fined by delaying the proceedings further than to once again say thank you to the Master and brethren of the Lodge, and to my personal host, Bro. . . . ."

Another example is this excerpt from a speech made by W. Bro. Rev. Herbert Dunnico, P.A.G.C. :—

(19) "I am not sure that we are as proud of Freemasonry as we ought to be. It is one of the most wonderful institutions in the world. Think of its historic past. Its roots are lost in the great abyss of time. Since it first came into existence, dynasties have disappeared, thrones have tottered, empires have vanished and crowns have crumbled, but our great order lives on with eye undimmed, greater, more powerful, more influential than ever. In days like these, when so many imagine that history only began with their own birth certificate, it is a fine thing to belong to an order with a great historic past. But if Masonry had only a great past, that would be no reason for pride. Our faith in Masonry is based upon the fact that it has a great mission to fulfil to the present age and a great contribution to make to the future of humanity. Here, within the Temple of Masonry, men differing in language, in modes of thought, in dress, and in habits of life, are able to meet around a common altar, share a common hope, and seek a common ideal. I am not sure that we Masons realise that Masonry is a progressive science. We are content to live on the fringe of the Order, we hug the shallows, and are afraid to launch out into the deep. We are prone to forget that night when we first saw the light of a new ideal, felt the thrill of a new inspiration and pledged ourselves to make a daily advancement in Masonic knowledge. The vision splendid fades

too often into the light of common day, and we go on year after year, unconscious of the fact that our strength is departing from us. This is the danger against which we Freemasons must ever guard.

"We Masons have a great task to perform. We are builders of a great city yet to be. Since the dawn of civilisation many cities have been built—some have been selfish and sordid, none have been perfect.

"Jerusalem has been termed the city of Faith, Rome the city of Law, Athens the city of Philosophy, and London the city of Liberty. There is one city yet to be built, the building of that city is our peculiar task, and the name of that city is 'This City of Fraternity'."

On one occasion the author was rather intrigued by the way in which a brother, replying for the visitors, made use of one sentence in the speech made by the proposer. In proposing the toast, the J.W. said that he felt that "if every member of the Craft brought the spirit of Masonry into his daily life the world would gradually become a better place to live in". In replying, the brother referred to, who was evidently an engineer, played upon the word "tolerance". Tolerances, he explained, were limits set by the designer of a machine or part, within which it was essential to keep, and the successful production of interchangeable machine parts depended upon careful inspection to ensure that all final dimensions were adhered to within defined limits or tolerances. Exact duplication in machinery was not possible, and still less possible in human nature, and what was wanted in the world to-day was greater tolerance in opinion, word and act. Freemasonry taught the exercise of tolerance in all things, and that was perhaps its greatest value to mankind.

Quite a simple note, applied naturally at somewhat greater length than is referred to here, which indicates an avenue open to anyone in making a speech, of drawing for inspiration upon that which they know best, viz., their daily avocation. The doctor, in like manner, could talk of hope and the spiritual message of healing which the Craft does not overlook; the accountant might refer to the importance of accuracy; the schoolmaster to the liberal arts and sciences; the builder to the square, etc.

In reading an account of an address on "Masonry Universal" delivered before the Manchester Association for Masonic Research, Mr. P. G. Jeffrey, who had visited lodges in all four quarters of the globe, referred to Cape Town as a fine example of Masonic co-operation. In that city, he said, there were twenty-nine Craft Lodges working together with splendid harmony, though they owed their allegiance to the Grand Lodges of England, Ireland and Scotland, and the Grand Orient of The Netherlands. Even in charity matters all four constitutions joined together. Furthermore, no Lodge would initiate a candidate unless his name had first been submitted to all the other Lodges to see if there was any brother who knew of any Masonic reason why the candidate should not be admitted.

Such a reference could quite well be introduced into a reply for "The Visitors," by using it as an example of the value of the Craft as a means of social intercourse wherever one was, and of indicating how the practice of admitting visitors tended to help to keep Masons in touch with the Craft wherever they were, and at the same time to broaden their minds by enabling them to see different rituals worked.

Many, in replying for the visitors, make some reference to the manner in which the W.M. and officers performed their work. There are, however, sometimes other items in connection with the visit to a Lodge which provide opportunity for comment. For example, the author once attended the second meeting of a new Lodge, and heard the Secretary read, as reported in the Minutes, the oration delivered by the Prov. G. Chaplain at the consecration of the Lodge. This provided a note on which to dwell in replying for the visitors later, by commenting upon the fact that it was pleasing to find such an item incorporated in the Minutes, and continued by saying that Secretaries should record in their Minutes such material as will make interesting history. What to-day may seem trivial and unimportant, may to-morrow or at some future date, have deep significance. A Lodge Secretary, holding office from year to year, as many do, has, or should have, a greater knowledge of the affairs and history of his Lodge than anyone else can have, and it should be possible from his records to write a full and complete history of the Lodge. By the aid of a supplemental scrap-book, he may preserve much valuable material that does not strictly fit into the recording of Minutes, but which in the compilation of a full history of the Lodge would be invaluable at a 21st, 50th or centenary celebration. Our present-day knowledge of old-time customs was largely based on well-recorded Minutes of early Lodges.

On another occasion the author remembers hearing a visitor recite the following lines, which were read at the funeral of a well-known American Mason, Bro. T. W. Hugo :—

(20)   Some time at eve, when the tide is low,
         I shall slip my moorings and sail away
         With no response to a friendly hail,
         In the silent hush of the twilight pale,
         When the night stoops down to embrace the day
         And the voices call in the water's flow—
         Some time at eve, when the water is low,
         I shall slip my moorings and sail away.
         Through purple shadows that darkly trail
         O'er the ebbing tide and the unknown sea,
         And a ripple of waters to tell the tale
         Of a lonely voyager, sailing away
         To mystic isles, where at anchor lay
         The Craft of those who had sailed before
         O'er the unknown sea to the unknown shore.

A few who watched me sail away
Will miss my craft from the busy bay ;
Some friendly barques what were anchored near,
Some loving souls that my heart held dear,
In silent sorrow will drop a tear
But I shall have peacefully furled my sail
In mooring sheltered from storm and gale
And greeting the friends who sailed before
O'er the unknown sea to the unknown shore.

He then referred to the impressively worked ceremony of a certain degree worked in Lodge that afternoon, and dwelt upon the value of friendships formed in the Craft and cemented in its Lodges.

It has already been said that reading helps in the preparation of speeches. The following is an example of a speech based upon two or three paragraphs in a book. "The Meaning of Masonry," by Bro. W. L. Wilmshurst :—

(21) "First let me express my gratitude for the welcome extended to all your visitors to-night. It has been said, and possibly some present have heard the comment made, that the working of our three degrees becomes monotonous, and that is why brethren come in late. Personally, I feel that while work is done in our Lodges, as it has been done in this Lodge to-day, when the Master and his officers concentrate as a team working to one end, viz., to impress the Candidate, those who listen and look on also gain useful lessons and have the importance of the tenets of our Craft impressed upon their minds. *Masonry, by means of a series of dramatic representations, is intended to furnish those who care to discover its purport and to take advantage of the hints it throws out in allegorical form, with an example and with instructions by which our return to the 'East' may be accelerated.*

From East to West the soul her journey takes,
At many bitter founts her fever stakes ;

> Halts at strange taverns by the way to feast,
> Resumes her load, and painful progress makes
>   Back to the East.

"In that journey we can find both refreshment and stimulation within the portals of a Masonic Lodge, and your visitors have appreciated the service you have rendered them in the work that has been done to-day." The lines in italics are taken from the book referred to.

Another example of a somewhat different kind is based upon a book "Edgar Wallace—Each Way," and after expressing thanks for hospitality received, the speaker might go on to say :—

(22) "Two outstanding features probably give me the greatest pleasure in Freemasonry. Firstly, I am able to meet many of varied occupations, ideals and social status on the level, and secondly, I feel I am working in an organisation which has a marked effect in building the characters of men. Probably all present know the name Edgar Wallace, even if some have not read his books or seen his plays. In a comment by Robt. G. Curtis, in a book 'Edgar Wallace—Each Way,' a biographical sketch, the following lines appear which provide a striking illustration of the effect of Masonry upon character. 'He may not have known much about the teachings of Wesley ; he may never have stood up in church and repeated a creed—I know of no creed which he could have repeated with perfect sincerity ; he may have failed utterly to realise that the destiny of his immortal soul depended on his choice between two doctrinal conceptions which differed by a hair's breadth ; but the golden rule of his life was based on the simple moral of 'Christie's Old Organ'—that one should always be kind to those who are less fortunate than oneself."

In effect one might add to the words of the biographer, he loved his fellow man, and never forgot the lesson taught on the day when he first saw Masonic Light, ever to be mindful of the needs of others. No one can attend a Lodge and not be further impressed with these important simple facts regarding life, and likewise all should be thankful for the opportunity so provided.

As the Master of a Lodge often finds himself called upon to reply when he visits another Lodge, the following outline speech may be of assistance.

(23) "It has been both pleasurable and profitable to sojourn among you tonight, and both for the pleasure and profit I have received I thank you, also appreciating the privilege of being here because it has enabled me to comply with the instructions given me at my installation. Those of you who have read accounts of the Craft Guilds in the Middle Ages will recall that before a Craftsman could become a Master he was required to make a tour of 'foreign' parts, working at his trade in order to gain a complete knowledge of his calling. Visiting still permits the Speculative Free-mason of this century to further his knowledge and exper-ience. From the lips of those who speak at the after-Lodge proceedings he often gains useful knowledge, as has been the case so far as your visitors are concerned to-night. From the working of the ceremonies he gains ideas on small points of difference, and that which he sees praise-worthy in others he can endeavour to emulate. To the Master of a Lodge it is undoubtedly an advantage during his year of office to be able to see the work done by others. Perhaps, that which has impressed me most this evening, is the evidence that there is a real soul in this Lodge. There are many institutions to-day possessing an admirable organisation, able to perform their allotted task without error and with perfect efficiency, but they lack what is meant by the word 'soul.' That is where I feel there is a difference in Freemasonry. While we have so many Lodges possessing real 'spirit' and 'soul,' there can be little risk of the Craft falling upon evil days, especially so in view of the fact that

each of our Institutions and our Hospital have the same distinguishing characteristic. I thank you not only for your hospitality, but also for the renewed vigour you have given me."

Naturally, no one wishes to be dull in after-dinner speaking, but there is some need to emphasise the fact that there is a difference between wit and vulgarity. That is why stories, or what some people term humour, must be handled with care and discretion. Freemasonry is a clean science, and rests upon a beautiful foundation; therefore, the superstructure should not be marred by the introduction of stories which do not tend to reflect beauty upon that superstructure. The speaker with a string of stories of doubtful merit, and still more doubtful value when appropriateness to the toast is concerned, may raise laugh after laugh, but he has merely acted as a comedian, and has contributed little or nothing to the lasting good of the Craft.

Those who are called upon to respond for the visitors can often exercise ingenuity by dealing with matters raised in the speech made by the brother who proposed the toast. This is not always the case, however, and sometimes little is said upon which one can comment. It is useful therefore to have at hand some quotations or outlines upon which to rely in case of need. A collection of useful phrases and quotations will be found at the end of this book.

9

LONDON AND OVERSEAS GRAND RANK

LONDON GRAND RANK

General Ideas.

Badge of honour—Encouragement to further efforts for the Craft—Conferred by the Grand Master following recommendation of P.M.'s of a Lodge—An honour founded in 1908 to provide a distinction for London brethren comparable to Provincial Grand Rank.

(24) TOAST OF THE BRETHREN OF LONDON GRAND RANK

"In asking you to drink to the health of the brethren of London Grand Rank, I would invite your attention to the fact that you will be honouring Past Masters of this and other Lodges, who have been given this distinction of Rank as a reward of merit, and following upon the recommendation of the Past Masters of their respective Lodges. It is by no means an honour to be treated lightly. The number of brethren so honoured each year is limited and the qualifications of these brethren are such that it must be admitted that they fully fulfilled their various duties as Masons and devoted much of their time to furthering the interests of the Craft. Neither must it be assumed that because these brethren are given no work to do of a ceremonial character in Consecrating new Lodges, they are a collection of brethren without a distinct entity. There is the London Rank Association, which apart from its work on behalf of charity, does much to maintain the interests of Past Masters in the Craft and provides a means of expressing collective opinion, when necessity arises."

(25)   CONGRATULATION ON APPOINTMENT TO
LONDON GRAND RANK [1]

"Brethren, I am very confident that it is a special pleasure to us all to offer to W. Bro. ————— our sincere congratulations on his being appointed. (By the M.W.G.M. to the rank of ————— in the Grand Lodge of England, or by the R.W. Provincial [or District] Grand Master for ————— to the rank of —— in that Province [or District]). This recognition of the many and devoted services rendered by our Brother to the Craft is especially gratifying to us, seeing our Lodge has the benefit of his knowledge of the Mystic Art, and his wise counsel and advice at all times. The honour reflects lustre on our Brother's reputation and adds to the prestige and credit of our Lodge. I, therefore, invite you to concur with my desire that there should be recorded on our minutes our gratification and pleasure at his appointment, and our hearty good wishes for a long enjoyment by our distinguished Brother of the honour now conferred upon him, which in our opinion is one he richly deserves."

(The foregoing would be a suitable resolution to be formally put and carried.)

(26) *Reply*.

"W.M. and Brethren, I am much affected by your kindness, and can only now offer you my most grateful thanks for your congratulations and good wishes I assure you, I deeply appreciate the honour conferred upon me, and this is enhanced by the cordial and fraternal reception you have given to me. Although of necessity my position will be more exacting, believe me there will be no difference in my feeling and actions towards you all, or slackening of my interests in and to the Lodge and its progress in time to come."

(If any presentation is made, suitable additions to the above will be found in later pages.)

(27)   CONGRATULATION ON APPOINTMENT TO
                    LONDON GRAND RANK [2]

"Bro. ————— : We rejoice to learn that the M.W.G.M.
has been pleased to appoint you to London Grand Rank.
It is indeed a double honour, for your name was first
selected by the Master and Past Masters of this Lodge for
submission to him, this being an honour conferred by your
Brethren of appropriate rank.   Secondly, the M.W. Grand
Master considered that recommendation, and your services
as stated therein justify him in conferring the rank upon
you.   It is true the appointment is to rank only and not to
an office, but you will realise that this places you in a position
of precedence, and is an indication to the whole Craft of
the good service you have rendered in the past.   For the
future, your rank will enable you to speak and act with
more certitude and authority.   May you be long spared to
enjoy the honour and to be with us to give your wise counsel
and advice and be an example of a Worthy Mason."

(If a resolution or presentation is made, the needful
additions can be found elsewhere in this book.)

(28) *Reply.*

"W.M. and Brethren, I tender you my very heartfelt
thanks for the kind and appreciative words you have
addressed to me.   It is very gratifying to me that the
M.W.G.M. has adopted the recommendation of the P.M.s
and conferred the honour upon me.   Believe me, I regard
it as setting the crown upon my rank as a P.M. and an
incentive to serve the Lodge and the Craft with renewed
energy and zeal."

(29)   LONDON GRAND RANK

"W.M., Officers and Brethren, There are three distinctive
points concerning London Grand Rank which particularly
attract my attention.   First, it is an honour conferred upon
Past Masters of London Lodges by M.W. the Grand

Master, as a reward of merit and an encouragement to further effort on behalf of the Craft we love so well. Secondly, the honour is only conferred by the M.W. the Grand Master after recommendation of a Brother has been made by his fellow Past Masters of the Lodge, men and Masons who have worked in Lodge with the recipient who know his merits and possibly his weaknesses. Thirdly, London is not only the hub of the British Commonwealth, but its historic name will for ever be writ large in the annals of the Craft, because the United Grand Lodge of England traces its origin to the meeting together of four old London Lodges which in 1717 set up a Grand Lodge to govern the Craft in London and its environs. To be entitled to wear the clothing appropriate to such rank is therefore no mean honour, and I not only appreciate it, but regard it as a useful reminder that there is still much work to be done in Masonry by Past Masters long after they have passed the Chair, and as I look around the Lodge and call to mind the enthusiasm of many others who I hope may live and progress to attain the same distinction."

(30) *Reply.*

"Worshipful Master, Officers and Brethren, In replying to the Toast of London Grand Rank, may I be permitted to say that London Grand Rank is conferred as an honour only by the Grand Master. It is also a Badge of Honour and an encouragement to further efforts on behalf of the Craft. London Rank was founded in 1908 to provide distinction for London Brethren comparable with Provincial Grand Rank. In passing, I should like to mention that the London Rank Association, apart from its work on behalf of Charity, does much to maintain the interests of Past Masters in the work of the Craft, and provides a means of expressing collective opinion when necessity arises.

In conclusion, I regard the conferment of London Grand Rank as setting the crown upon my rank as a P.M.

and a further incentive to serve the Lodge and the Craft with renewed energy and enthusiasm."

(31)   APPOINTMENT TO OVERSEAS RANK

"Brethren, For a long time Lodges such as our own, and there are many, situate far away from the centre of English Freemasonry and not controlled by any District Masonic Authority, had but few, if any, opportunities of the good work of any of its members being brought to the notice of, and being recognised by, the M.W.G.M. This has, you are no doubt aware, now been remedied by the institution of the honour of Overseas Rank, akin to that of London Grand Rank. It is my pleasing duty to inform you that our Bro. ———— has received the honour of Overseas Rank, and we join in offering him our congratulations upon that event, and our good wishes for his health and long enjoyment of the honour which is now his. In part that honour is ours also, for the prestige of our Lodge is increased by it. Bro. ————, we congratulate you sincerely and give you our heartiest good wishes."

(32) *Reply.*

"W.M. and Brethren, It is indeed very pleasant to receive your congratulations and good wishes on the additional rank to which I have been appointed. I am specially gratified by the fact that the work of Brethren so far away from the Home Country has been known to and recognised by our revered Grand Master. I appreciate your kindness and assure you of my continued support and interest in the Lodge."

If any formal resolution or a presentation follows, the foregoing can be amplified from other appropriate speeches, with any personal remarks suitable to the occasion.

10

SYMPATHY AND CONDOLENCE

(33)   ILLNESS OF A BROTHER

"Brethren, With great regret, I have to inform you that Bro. ————— has been laid by, suffering from (indicate nature of illness, or suggest its character), and, although I am told he is holding his own, he is in pain and very sadly. It is a time of great anxiety to his family and friends. It will surely by in accord with your wishes that Bro. Secretary should write in suitable terms to our Brother, expressing not only our sincere regrets, but also our fervent wishes for the early relief of his sufferings and recovery to complete health and strength. Let us not be content only with this, but remember each of us that kindly enquiries and words of personal sympathy and hope will console and encourage the sufferer. With your assent, I will arrange for a telegram being sent to our Brother expressing your good wishes and sympathy meanwhile."

(34)   IN TIME OF FAMILY ANXIETY

"Brethren, You will observe that Bro. ————— is not present, a circumstance so unusual that I venture to explain that owing to circumstances beyond his control, he and his family are passing through a time of considerable strain and anxiety. I have been made acquainted with the circumstances, and I am sure you will accept my assurance that Bro. ————— is not under any suggestion of adverse kind, but has acted, and will act, from the highest motives and intentions. Then, Brethren, I ask you to authorise my sending in your name our sympathy and good wishes to our Brother, and hopes for a happy conclusion to his present troubles."

(35)   ACCIDENT TO A BROTHER

"Brethren, We are all liable to accidents—some of us, perhaps, more than others. You will regret to hear that Bro. ———— has been in Hospital at ———— suffering from injuries caused by (state nature of accident). It is possible, I understand, that an operation may have to be performed. This naturally is of great concern to our Brother and his family, and I have asked Bro. (Almoner) to personally convey our regrets to the sufferer and his family, and to discreetly ascertain if we can add to our words some acts to show our sincerity, which may be welcome to enable them to cope with the calls upon them at this time of uncertainty. I need not propose a formal resolution, for I am persuaded your generosity and good feeling will dictate a willing concurrence."

(36)   CONDOLENCE ON DEATH OF A BROTHER

"Brethren, We have been warned in one of our ceremonies that a time will come, and the wisest of us knows not how soon when Death, the Great Leveller of all human greatness, will reduce us to the same state. This has been painfully exemplified by the death of our good Brother ————, for which reason we meet in the tokens of Masonic mourning. As you know, he was an active member of the Lodge (describe his activities, rank and services). His character marked him out as a worthy Brother, kind and generous, charitable in word and deed. We have lost a good friend and helpful Brother, but his example will remain with us as a cherished possession. Our condolences have been fittingly communicated to the relatives of our Brother and a floral token was deposited on his last resting-place in the name of the Lodge. You will, therefore, stand to order in solemn silence, as a tribute of respect to departed merit."

(If the Lodge was represented at the funeral, information might be given of that fact prior to the last paragraph foregoing.)

(37)   A Short Form

"Brethren, You are all aware that we mourn the death of
Bro. ————. He was a faithful Brother in the Craft,
always eager to take his part in its work and benevolence.
We realised, perhaps not fully, his worth and character, but
he was one whose place cannot easily be filled, but whose
influence and fraternal affection will avail as an example
to us all. Brethren, you will be upstanding in due form
and silence, as a tribute to his memory."

11

GOOD WISHES

(38)   To a Brother About to Take a
                    Long Journey

"Brethren. Before our next meeting, Bro. ————— will have left this country on a journey to (state place, object, and time of absence). It will be showing our affection and respect for him if, in your name and my own, I offer Bro. —————, as I now do, our united fraternal good wishes. May your journey, and temporary sojourn in distant parts, be pleasant and helpful to you, and your expectations of the result be amply realised. We wish you well, and may T.G.A.O.T.U. always have you in His keeping and bring you back once more to your home, your family, your friends, and your Brethren in safety, health and prosperity."

(39) *Reply*.

"W.M. and Brethren, I am gratified by, and thank you heartily for, your good wishes and kindly expressions. I shall recall them when far away with happy remembrances of your kindness. The nights of your regular meetings will evoke my thoughts of you all, and I shall know, too, that you have in me in mind. I hope in due time to meet you all again, and recount my doings and experiences. I again thank you all most sincerely."

(40)   To a Brother Leaving for Good

"Brethren, The intimation given by Bro. ————— of his desire (to become a country member, to resign, or as may be) calls for more than a formal acknowledgment. During his membership of the Lodge he has been a willing and helpful worker, and we have learned to respect and admire him. His present decision has been caused by (state reason, place of residence, or as may be). Bro. —————, we wish

you well ; may health, success and prosperity always attend
you, and happiness in your new sphere of life and action
be the reward of all your efforts. Keep in touch with us,
even if only now and then at regular intervals, and remember
our Absent Brethren toast, when we shall remember you.
A welcome will always await you, should circumstances
permit you to visit us, and now we needs must part, but
kindly feelings and our fraternal tie will remain to bind us
together still."

(41) *Reply*.

"W.M. and Brethren, No one could fail to appreciate the
kindly thought and feeling expressed by you towards me.
Still less myself, for they are the outcome of our association
together as members of this Lodge. Your good wishes are
especially helpful to me at this time, when so many intimate
relations are being severed. But the remembrance of all we
have been as Brethren, and your present kindliness will be
an inspiration to me in my future career. I thank you all
with the deepest gratitude."

(Other occasions for congratulation and good wishes can
be met from the terms of these and other appropriate
speeches elsewhere.)

(42)   CONGRATULATION ON BIRTH OF A LEWIS

"Brethren, I believe that in early times in Lodges—
certainly in some abroad—there was a ceremony of Baptism
or Adoption of a Lewis, the son of a Brother in the Lodge,
and the members were pledged to take an interest in the
child until it arrived at years of discretion. Such a procedure
is unknown in our Constitution now, but it is permissible,
and, indeed, in accordance with our principles, that we
should rejoice with a Brother on occasions of joy and
happiness. To Bro. ————— and his good wife a son has
been born, and I offer to them our collective congratulations
and sincere good wishes for the future health and progress

of the child. He is indeed a Lewis, properly so-called and as the symbol of a Lewis is strength, may this child become a strong link with his parents, a comfort and joy to them and a support in their declining years. In due time we may hope that he will become a Mason in this Lodge, and that his father may have the opportunity of initiating him and watching over his preliminary advances in the Craft."

(43) *Reply.*

"W.M. and Brethren, I thank you greatly for your congratulations and good wishes. The hopes you have expressed for our son's future will be an abiding inspiration in the days to come. May your anticipations be amply fulfilled and the light of Masonry be shed upon him in days yet far distant, to aid him in all the chances and changes of this transitory life, and his Brethren be to him a support and guide at all times."

12

APPRECIATION

(44)   APPRECIATION OF LONG SERVICE AS
                OFFICER, ETC. [1]

"Brethren, It has been said that the consciousness of
duty done is a great reward. It may be so, but services
rendered with no acknowledgment except a formal or
perfunctory word, may become irksome and merely matters
of rote or habit. This, however, is not the case with Bro.
————, who (state circumstances, such as the case
requires, long service in office, and the like).

During that time he has invariably carried out the duties
of his office faithfully and well. His fraternal and genial
manner towards all the Brethren, without distinction of rank
or position, his courtesy and tact, his unfailing attention to
detail, and ready devotion of time and energy, have been
actuated solely by his desire to advance the best interests of
the Lodge in every way possible. These qualities have
earned for him the admiration and respect—indeed, it is no
exaggeration to say the esteem and affection—of all his
Brethren.

"In order that those who succeed us in days to come may
find a record of our progress, and how much of it we owe
to the long, voluntary and devoted service of Bro. ————,
I have the pleasure to propose the following resolution to
be entered upon our minutes :—"

Let a resolution, in suitable terms, be seconded and put
to the Brethren for approval. If such a resolution only is
to form the recognition of the Brother's work, proceed as
follows :—

Additional remarks subsequently :

(45)   APPRECIATION OF LONG SERVICE AS
                  OFFICER, ETC. [2]

"Brother ———, The Brethren, by passing unanimously this resolution, have associated themselves openly in no formal or evanescent sentiments, which would be of little value, but have indicated their real feelings in an unmistakable manner. You have, indeed, heard all that has passed, and, although you are now, and must have been long previously, aware of our attitude towards you, yet we have now expressed our deep and sincere appreciation of, and thanks for, your long and disinterested work on behalf of the Lodge, and the affection of the Brethren for you. We wish you a continuance of health, strength and power to carry on for a long time to come. Little it is we have been able to do, but our sincerity will, we hope, make our wishes and thanks acceptable to you."

(46) *Reply.*

"W.M., and Brethren, Your generous and fraternal words and sentiments fill me with gratitude and pleasure. Pray accept my heartfelt thanks. The services I have been able to render to the Lodge and individual Brethren have been possible mainly because of the co-operation and accord which I have always received. My work has been to me a real labour of love. My reward truly has been as continuous as my service, for I have watched the progress and advancement of my Brethren as partly the result of my assistance and advice. You can hardly realise the depth of my feelings as I saw a long succession of Officers and Masters working with advantage to the Lodge and to the Craft. I shall always regard today's proceedings as an incentive to continue, as long as I am able, the work which you have recognised in such generous terms."

(47)   APPRECIATION OF WORK FOR BENEVOLENCE

"Brethren, The report which has just been made by Bro.
——————— in reference to the benevolence of the Lodge and
Brethren during the past year, must have aroused and stirred
your feelings. There is no need for me to dwell on the
amount we have raised, or to go into details to show how
they compare with the figures of any other year. I do not
regard with approval any attempt to beat a record, for such
an idea is repugnant to the true spirit of benevolence. I do,
however, compliment you on the continued interest you
have shown in our benevolent work, and the warm-hearted
support you have given during a period of peculiar difficulty.
It would not, however, be right for me to make no reference
to the endeavours of Bro. ——————— (our Almoner, or as
may be). He has made himself, once more, responsible for
carrying out the work of collection and securing donations
and subscriptions. In doing so he has applied energy, tact,
and tenacity to his task, which has assured the success of
our endeavours, and ensured the least possible inconvenience
or trouble to those who have given their support to our
projects. Bro. ———————, for your efforts and assistance, we
owe you our grateful thanks, which we now tender to you
in ample measure."

(48) *Reply.*

"W.M. and Brethren, I am gratified by your appreciation
of what has been done in the cause of benevolence.
(Mention, if need be, any particular part of the work needing
special reference.) The Brethren, I am sure, have always
been actuated by the true spirit, and, without narrow views
on the subject, have with open, generous hearts, responded
to my invitations to subscribe and assist in the good work.
For myself, my reward is the success of our exertions, the
benefit to the objects of our benevolence, and, not least,
the goodwill and appreciation of you all."

(49)   A SHORTER FORM, APPLICABLE TO A
                        STEWARDSHIP LIST

"Brethren, You are aware that I represented the Lodge
at the recent Festival of the ——— Institution. The list
realised £——— and no fewer than ——— of you acted
as Stewards. The result is most gratifying. The reputation
of the Lodge for its unfailing support of the Masonic
Institutions has been fully maintained. I sincerely trust our
success will keep bright one of the greatest ornaments of
our Craft and will be an incentive to your interest and
support in the future. We are all much indebted to Bro.
——— for his invaluable services in connection with the
list and the collection and transmission of the donations.
His work has proved his energy and we thank him heartily."

(50) *Reply.*

"W.M. and Brethren, It is a kindly thought which
prompted our Master to mention my name in connection
with our joint effort. Truly, I am grateful and offer to
him and you my best thanks. The success we have attained
has been achieved by the efforts of all. Especially valuable
has been the Benevolent Association, which has enabled all
its members to make small but regular contributions, so
that there has been no large claim at one moment to act
possibly as a detriment to ourselves or our connections. I
hope that those Brethren who are not members of the
Association will join it without delay in preparation for our
next effort."

(51)   TO A BROTHER FOR ORGANISING
                      A SOCIAL FUNCTION

"Brethren, I think it only right to make a short reference
to the recent (Outing, Ball, Gold Match, Ladies' Festival,
or other function should be shortly described). All who
were present at the function expressed their enjoyment and
pleasure. There are those who regard such events as

unnecessary in connection with the Craft, but, as I view them, we give pleasure in this way to others besides ourselves, we cement old friendships and create new associations, and produce a feeling of harmonious pleasure between members of the Craft and those not of our Fraternity. This has certainly been the case in our latest venture. The successful result has been mainly due to the untiring efforts of Bro. ———— and the Committee acting with him. We offer to him and his associates our grateful thanks for all the trouble and care they took on our behalf."

(52) *Reply.*

"W.M. and Brethren, On behalf of the Committee and myself, I thank you for your appreciation of our efforts. Our work was rendered light and pleasant by the friendly co-operation of all concerned. Without exception, everyone contributed to the result which you have so rightly described. We have made many new friends, and no expression of dissatisfaction has been heard. We thank you all."

(53) To the Organiser of a Presentation

"Brethren, The presentation which has just been made (to Bro. ————, the Lodge, or as the case may be) has given us all pleasure and satisfaction, and it may rightly be termed an indication of our fraternal interest and association, which will remain long after to-day's ceremony. The suggestion of making the presentation came from Bro. ————, who is ever anxious that proper and friendly action should be taken in any way which unity of thought and consideration be indicated. To him fell the duty of organising and carrying into effect the scheme now so fully materialised. The result is such that we cannot fail to realise how much we are indebted to Bro. ———— for all the work he has done with so much energy, tact and attention to detail and propriety. On your behalf, I offer to him our best thanks for his work and thought in this connection."

(54) *Reply.*

"W.M. and Brethren, The final result of the presentation is now fully apparent, and while it is pleasant and satisfactory, it is not surprising.   So far as I am concerned, I had no fears on the subject, for as time went on the many kindly expressions of assent, offers of help, advice and suggestions, combined to make my task a light and pleasant one.   For your thanks and appreciation, I am more than obliged—indeed, I am delighted, and grateful to you all."

13

PRESENTATIONS AND DEDICATION

(55)   PRESENTATION OF CERTIFICATE

"Bro. ————, It gives me much pleasure to present to you, as I now do, the Certificate of your having been regularly made a Master Mason according to the Constitutions of the United Grand Lodge of England. You will realise that it is the evidence of your position and rank as a Mason, and, therefore, a precious document of which you should take a special care. It is the visible bond between the Craft and yourself, for on the one hand it bears the seal of Grand Lodge and the signature of the Grand Secretary to indicate on their part that you are entitled to the great and invaluable privileges of the Craft while you obey its regulations. On the other hand, it will, in a few moments, bear your signature (which must never be varied) to show your adherence to those Constitutions and the pledges you have given during your Masonic progress. To aid you in this, let me point out to you some of the symbols on the certificate. The three columns represent Wisdom, Strength and Beauty, typifying the results expected from your life and actions. Your work should be inspired by Wisdom, carried out with Strength, and result in Beauty, an adornment to the inward man, but recognisable by those who observe your actions and yourself. The V. of S.L. and other emblems you are acquainted with, but, finally, I may direct your attention to the Tracing Board, the symbol of your life, upon which you should trace well-ordered and well-formed lines, or you may only produce badly-formed or devised lines, according as you have followed or departed from the principles already mentioned. Remember! one day, we know not how soon, or how long delayed, you will be summoned to the Grand Lodge Above, there to present your life's Tracing Board to T.G.A.O.T.U., by whose unerring and impartial justice your work will be judged. May that judgment be as favourable to you as it will be merciful.   So mote it be."

(56)   A Shorter Form of Presentation

"Bro. A.B., I present to you the Grand Lodge Certificate of your being a Master Mason, duly made according to our regulations.   It is important that you should preserve it carefully, being part, and a most necessary part, of the evidence which will be needed to vouch you, should you visit strange Lodges, or desire to become a Joining Member of another Lodge, or to become a member of the Order of the Royal Arch.   Do not display it as a picture or advertisement, for that would belittle the Craft and yourself.   Let me invite your study of the emblems displayed on the Certificate and their open and symbolic meaning.   When your signature has been added, you will be fully equipped as a Mason, and we look forward with confidence to your advancement in Masonic knowledge and continued progress in the Craft."

(57)   A Short, Formal Address

"Bro. ————, I present you with the Grand Lodge Certificate, to which you are now entitled.   You should sign it in the space indicated in order that it may be completed.   Take care of it, and remember you may be called upon to produce it when you are visiting another Lodge, or on other necessary occasions, as evidence of your identity and rank as an English Master Mason."

(58)   Presentation of a P.M. Jewel

"Brethren, It has been an age-long custom in the Craft to present a Jewel to the Immediate Past Master of the Lodge at the earliest opportunity after the cessation of his year of office as Master of the Lodge.   This old and laudable custom enables the Brethren to ensure the possession by him of a graceful and beautiful token of their appreciation of his services in the Chair, and in the work of the Lodge, and the preservation of the rights and privileges of the Brethren. This token he can wear with pleasure, possibly also with pride, on all proper Masonic occasions. W.Bro. —————, actuated by such sentiments, I now present to you this Jewel. (Does so.) You will observe that it bears (make any apt reference to the device or inscription on the Jewel) the Master's Square, from which depends the badge of a P.M. I need not explain these to you, but they represent the advances in power and knowledge which you as a P.M. and Ruler in the Craft have made. We earnestly hope you will long be with us to wear the Jewel, and be an example of what a worthy Mason is, and should be. We thank you for all you have done, the ideals you have upheld, the principles and tenets you have exemplified, and we have every confidence that your interest in and help to the Lodge will never wane."

(59) *Reply* [1].

"W.M. and Brethren, The presentation of this very beautiful Jewel, accompanied by your moving eloquence, and the high appreciation and hopes you entertain in regard to myself, fill me with gratitude and pleasure too deep for words. Could I adequately, but voicelessly, transfer to you my feelings at this moment, you would realise with what pride and satisfaction I regard your gift and speech. But I can only ask you to accept my simple, but heartfelt, 'Thank you!' I shall never forget the year I served you as Master, for he rules best who serves most ; nor shall I fail to recall your kindly appreciation of what I have done. Little or much, as the work has been, it was the outcome of my earnest and sustained desire to uphold the traditions of the Lodge, and to worthily follow in the steps of my predecessors. The inevitable feeling of regret which is caused by leaving the Chair has been replaced by your fraternal kindness, and has created a strong desire to serve you still more. This shall be the ideal, as well as the mainspring, of all my endeavours in the future."

(60) *Reply* [2].

"Bro. ————, I tender hearty thanks for the Jewel presented to me. In looking back over the work of the past year, I am amazed at the great amount accomplished. Those results are such that few Lodges, if any, have surpassed or even equalled. I feel greatly honoured to have been your Master, but the results are the cumulative effect of the efforts of all and we have a right to be proud, a pride which excludes boasting, but which acts as an incentive to bigger efforts in the future. It is my sincere desire and hope that the Lodge will keep in sight the high ideals of the Craft—the practice in everyday life of Brotherly Love, Relief, and Truth, against which there is no law in heaven or earth, but by which power and the highest prosperity are certain. I trust I have done something, if ever so little, to encourage emulation in the realm of high personal and Masonic endeavour. Amidst all the unrest and false teachings of the day, the foundation of the Craft stands as firm as a rock. Brotherly Love, Relief and Truth will always prevail, and it is in times of uncertainty that the fundamental principles of Masonry are so much needed. Proclaiming again that the greatest pleasure in life is not getting but giving ; giving for a Brother's necessity, giving up anything short of principles to secure truth, peace and concord ; glorying in the success of others—in one word, the conscientious constant practice of unselfishness. If by repeating that truth I have raised your ideals of the Craft, I am truly satisfied. Masonry for each of us is exactly what we make it, the directing impelling power within us. We can make it an instrument of almost unbounded good to ourselves and those around us, while failure to understand its true meaning reduces the Craft to that Brother to the level of a club. Keep our ideals high, let the Grand

Principles permeate the spring of life, then conduct will be like a stream of pure water, spreading sweetness and growth wherever it touches."

(61)   ANOTHER FORM OF PRESENTATION,
         APPLICABLE TO SPECIAL CASES

"W.Bro. ———, The Brethren of the Lodge having unanimously voted the presentation to you of a Past Master's Jewel, I am happy to have the privilege of handing it to you. (Does so.) We are all aware that, owing to adverse circumstances (describe them, such as ill-health, absence abroad, or as may be), it has not been possible for you to be with us, or to perform all the ceremonies, on every occasion of our meeting. But you have shown to us the true Masonic spirit—good work done in the face of difficulties, a kindly interest in every member of the Lodge, and a patient endurance in trouble. These have made a deep impression on us all, and one more lasting than mere ritual service only. We rejoice to have you with us to-night, and wish you health and strength to enable you to be our associate, friend and Brother for many years to come."

(12) *Reply*.

"W.M. and Brethren, With feelings of intense gratitude I receive this Jewel, which I shall always prize as a special token of your goodwill. The high hopes I formed of service to you when I was elected to the Chair have, to my infinite regret, not been wholly realised. In the face of adverse circumstances, known to you all, I did what I could, buoyed up by the knowledge of your forbearance and consideration. Even when absent, I had you in thought, with hopes for a brighter future. I thank you all most sincerely. Your kindness and good wishes will be an ever-present memory, and an incentive to the fullest service in the future I am able to give. At least that will be my strong desire and constant aim."

(63)   A Short Form

"W.Bro. —————, It is with considerable satisfaction, but some regret, that I present to you the Jewel of a P.M. of the Lodge. (Does so.) Satisfaction, because the completion of your year of office has given us the opportunity of giving you a tangible token of our appreciation and regard. Regret, because you will not continuously rule over us, except at occasional intervals. Your year has been eminently pleasant and fruitful of good to us all."

(64) *Reply*.

"W.M. and Brethren, I give you my hearty thanks for this Jewel, which I shall wear with great satisfaction and pleasure. As the years go by I shall still regard your gift with the same feelings, and it will help me to carry out my desire to be of the utmost service to the Lodge and the Craft I love so well."

(65)   On a Gift of Masonic Clothing

"Brethren, At comparatively infrequent intervals some important Masonic honour is conferred upon a member of our Lodge, and these provide an opportunity for ourselves to add to that honour by such means as are usual or available in the particular instance. We rejoice in unison to-night, for Bro. ————— has been appointed (to Grand Lodge office or rank, London, Provincial District or other rank, as may be). Therefore, to you, Bro. —————, and in accordance with the unanimous wish of your Brethren, I offer our congratulations on the appointment and our hearty good wishes for your future service and progress. We fully acknowledge how well deserved are your new honours, and we regard them as reflecting honour on the Lodge. To signalise the event, and add to our pleasure, we now present to you the complete clothing and Jewels of your new position in Masonry, asking your acceptance of them as a token of our pride and satisfaction, as well as of our hope that you will live long to enjoy the distinction conferred upon you."

(Invest, if entitled, with the Regalia, or hand it to the Brother.)

(66) *Reply*.

"W.M. and Brethren, I am overwhelmed by your generous gift and the cordial expressions which have accompanied it. I fully concur with your remarks and can assure you that the honour conferred upon me by (the M.W.G.M., or as may be) is enhanced by the knowledge that, in a sense, the Lodge shares it with me. In olden times a signal honour was conferred upon an individual by some great Sovereign, by means of a Robe, Chain, or other object but here the honour comes from one hand, and the gift from my Brethren, who are on the same level, regulated by the same Square, and circumscribed by the same Compass as myself. Hence my unalloyed pleasure and gratitude. My new rank carries to me the call for greater service, which I shall adopt willingly and hopefully, for the advantage of the Lodge, my Brethren, and the Craft at large."

(67)   ON GIFT TO THE LODGE

"W.M. and Brethren, For some time past I have contemplated making a gift to the Lodge to mark (state reason actuating gift). I have decided that a suitable gift would be (name it with a special description needful). I ask you to accept this gift on behalf of the Lodge, to be used on all proper and suitable occasions, in remembrance of the many heart-warm friendships formed and retained in the Lodge, and to remind the Brethren now here, and those to come after, that the object of our Institution is to be happy and communicate happiness. May this be the result, and may the gift aid to recall the days that are past, and be a bright augury of those yet to come."

(68) *Reply.*

"Bro. ————, On behalf of the Lodge, I accept your gift, so aptly chosen and well designed to carry out and illustrate your intentions. In offering you our cordial thanks, I can only say that your words and actions are typical of the fraternal spirit you have always evinced, both in and out of the Lodge. May the use of the (name gift) inspire our members to ever seek for the highest good, and the noblest ideals, which our Fraternity affords, and, further, to act upon our principles and tenets to the fullest extent towards Brethren and all men, in the manner you have exemplified at all times."

(Resolution in formal terms might follow; if so, a formal acknowledgement would suffice.)

(69) A LODGE BANNER

"W.M. and Brethren, The Lodge having been recently consecrated, the Founders and donors of the gift have collaborated to present to the Lodge a Banner of a suitable and befitting character, for the adornment and use of the Lodge. On behalf of the donors, it is my privilege to invite your acceptance of the Banner about to be unveiled by (name and rank of Brother to do this), and I suggest to you that our Brother the Chaplain (or as may be) should then appropriately dedicate the Banner to the use of the Lodge, and, above all, to the glory of T.G.A.O.T.U., without whose divine and special favour all our works are of no avail."

(Unveiling of Banner.)

(70) ACCEPTANCE BY THE W.M.

"Bro. ————, With the most lively feelings of satisfaction and pleasure I accept, on behalf of the Lodge, the Banner now presented and unveiled. I invite our Bro. Chaplain (or as may be) to offer up suitable dedicatory prayers and invocations as may seem to him appropriate for the occasion, in order that the gift may be always set apart from profane purposes, and reserved only for Masonic use."

(Dedication by the Chaplain.)

(71)   ADDRESS AFTER DEDICATION

"Brethren, We have now seen the completion of a ceremony which will have an effect deep and lasting—indeed, continued while the Banner now presented and dedicated is in being, or our record of the proceedings remains. We shall desire to place on our minutes an acknowledgment (to Bro. ——————— and the donors) of our indebtedness and thanks for this beautiful gift. The spirit of unity and concord, of wisdom and beauty, and of true craftsmanship is demonstrated before us in this Banner. May it ever remind us of the fraternal affection which does, and ever should, animate Masons in all places and at all times. May the symbols illustrated upon it lead us to seek the highest ideals and direct our actions in harmonious relations with all men, and enable us to prove to the world the happy and beneficial effects of our Ancient and Honourable Institution."

(72)   ON GIFT OF A V. OF S.L.

"W.M. and Brethren, It is with deep and sincere feeling that I present to the Lodge this V. of S.L., which, I trust, will be used in our proceedings henceforth. It is not only a symbol of our belief in T.G.A.O.T.U., and an integral element in the completeness and propriety of our meetings but it constitutes the primary irremovable landmark of our Craft. (If it is an ancient copy, or of special interest, detail thus.) Thus, W.M. and Brethren, I place this Holy Book in your charge, being full persauded that your knowledge of all that it is to Masons and Masonry will ensure its honourable preservation and use as one of the most valued possessions of the Lodge."

(73) *Reply.*

"Bro. —————, Your gift, so generously presented in such moving and eloquent terms, is gratefully accepted by the Lodge and all of its members.   The high tone of your remarks, indicative, as they are, of your thoughts and desires, will inspire us to view this V. of S.L. with even greater honour, regard and appreciation than before. Indeed, the Sacred Volume is given to us not only as the rule and guide of our Faith, but it is the unerring standard by which to regulate our own thoughts, words and actions, as well to our neighbours, but greatest of all, our duty to God. While we are conversant with the contents of the Sacred Volume and adherent to its precepts, we shall be enabled to carry out our duties as Men and Masons with fervency and zeal."

14

AFTER CEREMONY OF CONSECRATION

(74)   OF THANKS TO CONSECRATING OFFICERS

"Brethren, Our Lodge is now fully constituted, and our hopes in this respect have been amply realised. We are now, it is true, the newest and least of the stones in the stately and superb edifice of Masonry, but I am sure you realise, as I do, that as an integral part of that edifice we have laid upon us the duty of fulfilling the destiny of the Craft, and of bearing our share of its burdens, while sharing in its glories. Thus it is that to-day's ceremony, so beautiful in its nature, and rendered with such graceful charm and dignity, fills us with gratitude to the Consecrating Officers and for all their care in fitting us to begin and consummate the work for which this Lodge is designed. We are not, nor could we be, critics of, or pass judgment upon, what we have seen and heard, but our feelings call on us to offer our most sincere and grateful thanks for all they have done and for the fraternal attitude and kindness they have shown towards us. I therefore move (Resolution of thanks in appropriate terms, seconded formally, and carried). W.M. to Consecrating Officer : V.W.Bro. (or as may be), Pray accept for yourself and your colleagues the thanks of the Brethren of the ———— Lodge as formally expressed by the resolution just passed, but as a sincere expression of our gratitude we ask you to accept this ———— as a small memento of the occasion, and we invite you to add to our indebtedness to you all by accepting Honorary Membership of the Lodge just being brought into being by your aid. We are assured that with your names at the head of our Roll of Members, we shall ever be mindful of the duty of so acting at all times as to fully justify the high hopes and anticipations entertained for the future progress of the Lodge."

(Reply by C.O. and election.)

(75)   OF THANKS TO ORGANISERS OF
                NEW LODGE

"Brethren, The work connected with the formation of the Lodge and of carrying out the varied details and preparations, concluding with to-day's ceremony, has mainly fallen upon Bro. ————. He has done his part nobly and well, never failing to meet all difficulties with tact and fraternal consideration. On your behalf, I extend to him our thanks and appreciation of his work, and we more than ever realise that we shall for all time remain his debtor."

(If given in Lodge, a resolution might be added.)

(76) *Reply*.

"W.M. and Brethren, Your thanks and appreciation are very gratefully accepted by me. I rejoice that all the efforts made, supported at all times by the Founders and yourself, have resulted in the complete success of to-day's ceremony. Let us not be content, Brethren, but remember we are now beginning a career which, I trust, will be successful, full of good works, and instinct with the principles and tenets of the Craft which it is now our duty to exemplify at all times. That we shall do this and the Lodge become a shining light in the Masonic world, is my earnest prayer and confident hope."

(77)   OF THANKS TO SUPPORTERS AND DONORS

"Brethren, it is only right and courteous that we should not omit to express our thanks for the very cordial support and assistance rendered in regard to the formation of the Lodge by the W.M., Wardens and Brethren of the ———— Lodge, No. —, who took into consideration the circumstances and reasons giving rise to our action, and gave their willing assent and support to our Petition for the Warrant, and have maintained their interest in our doings. Then various presents have been made to the Lodge as the outcome of the fraternal zeal and affection of the Brethren. (The names of donors and nature of gifts might be stated.) To each of these Brethren we give our hearty thanks, and our assurance that we shall at all times value the gifts and honour the givers."

If time does not permit the last two speeches in Lodge, they might be given after the dinner, or at a subsequent meeting.

Replies need be only formal or spontaneous.

(78)   THANKS TO FOUNDERS

"Brethren, The fact that we have now been fully and legally constituted as a Lodge, under the United Grand Lodge of England, indicates the completion of the work of founding the Lodge. To all the Brethren who as Founders participated in the work, with willing hearts and ready hands, I offer my sincere thanks—none the less sincere because my remarks are halting and incomplete. Brethren, together we have laid a Foundation strong, broad and well compacted. Upon that Foundation we have to erect a superstructure, perfect in its parts and honourable to the Builders. That is now our task. Like the Masons of old-time, we may not see the completion of the stately and superb edifice we have designed, but with due care and judgment, by zeal and assiduity, and conscious of the aid of T.G.A.O.T.U., let us go on and strive to excel, and success will attend our efforts."

(79) *Reply*.

"W.M., on behalf of the Founders, I tender to you our appreciation of your thanks and our accord with the high principles you have indicated for our future guidance. We cannot, and do not desire to appropriate to ourselves all the credit and praise for the formation of the Lodge. We were inspired and animated by your words and example, and carried out such parts of the work as were allotted to us with an enthusiasm and spirit created by you. We are profoundly glad that the end had justified our exertions. In the succeeding work we shall follow your lead in the same spirit and you may rely on our aid and example at all times."

(80   PRESENTATION TO FIRST MASTER

"W.M., There has been allotted to me the privilege of addressing you on behalf of the Founders (and members) of this Lodge. We are desirous of offering to you our congratulations and good wishes on the (close of your year of office as the First Master of the Lodge, or as may be). You have held up to us a high Masonic ideal, true service, and the most fraternal spirit, which we realise will be our duty to strive for and maintain. When we elected you for nomination as Master-Designate, we had the fullest confidence in you, and the sincerity of your principles, and we expected from you the creation of a standard of action which those who come after you could follow with high and uplifted feelings of regard and affection. You have realised all our hopes, justified our expectations, and we look forward to your counsel, advice and assistance in the future whenever needed. As a tangible token of our gratitude to you and of our love and affection for you, I ask your acceptance of this (name and describe gift), which we hope you will long regard with satisfaction and value, as well for intrinsic worth, as for our sincere good will towards you."

(If presented in Lodge, a resolution might be proposed and carried.)

(81) *Reply.*

"W.Bro. ————, To your associated Founders and Brethren, and no less to yourself as their representative,

I offer my heartfelt thanks for this gift, so beautiful and so indicative of the object you have in view. I cannot disguise from myself that my words are an inadequate expression of my feelings, which I would fain make more apparent to you. The occasion for the gift is one which gives opportunity for associating your efforts with my own in the great work we undertook. Without your fraternal consideration and aid I could not have made progress or directed our efforts to a favourable and successful conclusion. Your gift will be a constant reminder of our work together, and of the friendly attitude you have always adopted towards me. I thank you sincerely for the gift and the kindliness which dictated its presentation. (If the gift were a Loving Cup, or other article capable of use at Lodge Dinners, and the Donee were so minded, continue : In order that all the Brethren of the Lodge may have this reminder constantly before them, and be able to share in the pleasure of the use of the gift, I am desirous of presenting it to the Lodge, in whose care and protection it may be kept and used on all appropriate occasions. To me this will be the most fitting method of perpetuating the splendid sentiments which have inspired you all.)"

15

THE WORSHIPFUL MASTER

GENERALLY speaking the task of proposing this toast is entrusted to the Immediate Past Master, and this duty will devolve upon him on at least four occasions, and in some Lodges seven or eight times. Thinking ahead is, therefore, advantageous ; one does not want to explode all one's ideas at the first or second effort, and be left devoid of points of interest for ensuing meetings. Unfortunately, this toast, and its reply, too often consist of an over-liberal exchange of compliments between the Master and the I.P.M. One should naturally be willing to notice and encourage that which is praiseworthy in others, but too much sweetness can lead to nausea on the part of those who have to swallow the mixture.

General Ideas.

Placed in position to control Lodge by vote of brethren—Confidence in their choice—Sincerity a distinct point in his work—Will maintain traditions set by predecessors—Possessed of tact and ability to control—Zealous for progress of Lodge—Kindly way of encouraging others marks him as a leader—Stalwart supporter of the L. of I. now has opportunity of proving value of studies.

(82)   Toast to the W.M. [1]

"It has given me very great pleasure to install you as Master of this Lodge, and I have risen with probably greater pleasure to propose this toast, because it enables me to express a few words to the brethren concerning yourself. In electing you to your present honoured position the brethren have shown confidence in you as a leader, feeling sure that the ability, tact, judgment and zeal which you

have already displayed will enable you to discharge the
duties of your office with credit to yourself and to the Lodge.
Your period of office will last for twelve months.   Not
long ago you represented the setting sun in the West.
To-night, we find you as the rising sun in the East with all
its glory and splendour ; its promise of that which is good
to come, and before the time comes for you to pass on,
making way for someone else, I feel confident your record
will be a wealth of good accomplished.   Your period in the
chair, being limited in duration, points out that useful
lesson to all of us, that we must perform our allotted task
within due time.   It is my duty to express on behalf of
every member of the Lodge our heartfelt confidence in you
and our sincere wishes for a very happy period of office to
which we know you have looked forward for many years.
Any assistance we can give you will be happily rendered."

(83)   TOAST TO THE W.M. [2]

"Once again I rise to propose the toast of our W.M.
His period of Mastership is almost half over.   At the present
time he is like the noonday sun at the meridian, radiating
the maximum of light and energy for the benefit of us all.
We can say that real progress has been made, and that not
only the candidates, but also the members of the Lodge
have gained considerable benefit from the very sincere way
in which he has rendered the ceremonies.   Of course, being
modest, he will probably attribute a large measure of his
success to the officers and others, but it must be borne in
mind that he takes the lead, and it is his pleasant way of
encouraging everyone which has so largely contributed
toward the marked evidence of the team spirit in the working
of the ceremonies.   He has and is doing his part, but before
I conclude this speech, I will ask the question—Are we all
doing our share ? By that I mean has everyone who can,
without detriment to himself and connections, made some
personal sacrifice of a little pleasure, in order to ensure

that the list the Master is taking up for the ———— Institution, shall be worthy both of the Lodge, and of his great interest in the work that body carries out ? That is, after all, the most effective way in which we can show our appreciation for the work he has so ably performed for the benefit of the Lodge."

(84)   TOAST TO THE W.M. [3]

"Brethren, The toast I have to propose is one that will be received with acclamation. For me to dismiss the toast by saying it will fall to my lot on several occasions in future to propose his health would not be fulfilling but evading a traditional duty of the I.P.M. I am sure that you have put in the Chair a Brother who is going to uphold the high traditions which the Lodge has already attained. When I was at school I was taught the English language was largely built up on the vowels—a, e, i, o, u. I feel this evening those could be aptly applied to the W.M. in this sense : A, ability ; E experience ; I, integrity ; O, opportunity ; and U, unselfishness. I am sure the W.M. has all these qualities. Our united wishes go out to him this evening, in the hope that his year of office will be one that will ever remain green in his memory."

(85)   TOAST TO THE W.M. [4]

"Brethren, It seems but yesterday I was installed, yet a year has passed and another enjoys that high honour. From time immemorial such has been the custom in Freemasonry, a very salutary custom it is, as it prevents any freehold in the Master's Chair, and ensures freshness and variety of ideas and practice, thus keeping the Craft ever young, and encouraging each Brother to strive to perfect himself and eventually become capable of reigning as Master of his Lodge. To-night we greet our new ruler, a Brother who has gained for himself the respect and love of the whole

Lodge, by his straight-forward, consistent and honourable
conduct. We have pledged ourselves to support him,
feeling assured that his leading will always be for the good
of Freemasonry in general and this Lodge in particular.
I am certain that in all difficulties the W.M. will shine.
We can feel quite safe under his guidance, and have every
confidence in his judgment. In all his work for the Lodge
the W.M. can rely upon the steady and full support of all.
We can look forward to a great year, and I assure you, Bro.
————, of the undivided cordial support of each Past
Master, Officer and Member of the Lodge."

(86)   Toast to the W.M. [5]

"So quickly does time fly, that it does not seem very long
ago that, speaking on behalf of the members of the Lodge,
I welcomed you as a new ruler in the Craft, and as the
Master of this Lodge. Now your work in that capacity is
nearly completed. This will be the last evening during
which you will preside at the festive board. Whilst, therefore, you can possibly visualise the sun setting at the end
of your day of authority, I would indicate to you that
Masonry, being a progressive science, it is but natural that
you should in due time hand over the gavel to another.
That will not mean, however, that your days of active work
in the Craft are ended. We in this Lodge do not allow our
P.M.s to become extinct volcanoes, and the able manner in
which you have discharged your duties has been too pro-
nounced for the Brethren to look upon you as being an
ornament on the shelf. The new Master will extend to
you the appreciation of the Lodge after you have installed
him, but, speaking as your I.P.M. for presumably the last
time, I would like to conclude by saying that the confidence
the Brethren placed in you has certainly not been misplaced,
and in the years to come you should be able to look back
upon this year with pride and pleasure as a period well
spent, and a task well done."

(87)   REPLY BY THE W.M. [1]

"W.Bro. ————, I thank you for the way you have proposed the toast and for the all-too-generous terms in which you have mentioned the qualities I am supposed to possess. I also thank the Brethren for the way they have received the toast. To me this occasion is unique in my life-time. I am conscious of the fact that my predecessors in this Chair have set a very high standard, which one would try to emulate. Although the standard has been set high, I am not dismayed but inspired by it. I shall strive as far as I can to maintain and uphold the dignity of the Lodge, and so far as in me lay to rule it with sympathy—as it should be ruled. I shall endeavour to give you as much as I possibly can of what I believe to be the true principles of Masonry. I am not here to formulate a programme. I am conscious of this fact—that Freemasonry is something more than a Creed, something more than a Curriculum, something more than a mere system of thought. We are taught that the first preparation for Masonic life is in the heart. If you, in your hearts, are prepared to receive Freemasonry, I am sure that in the Lodge nothing will be found wanting. If at the end of my year of office I am able to hand over without any spot or blemish the charter, pure and unsullied as I received it, if I should have gained a little place in the affectionate regard of my Brethren, if I should have been able to inculcate in you a loftier idea and higher standard of Freemasonry, then whatever sacrifices the labours of the year might entail for me, I feel I shall pass out to the reward I hoped and lived for, the thought that my life in the Lodge has not been in vain."

(88)   REPLY BY THE W.M. [2]

"Bro. ————, I am very pleased to be the Master of this Lodge. It is one of the chief events of my life. I will endeavour to do all that is expected of me, and to the satisfaction of the members. I hope for the support of the

Officers and Brethren, and with that nothing will be lacking on my part to make the Lodge a success."

(89)   REPLY BY THE W.M. [3]

"I am naturally proud to be the —th Master of the Lodge, a fact which, if possible, still further brings home to me the responsibilities which every member owes to the Craft as a whole and to this Lodge in particular. As each year passes by, and each new Master is installed, the Lodge starts a new era with all its possibilities and its pitfalls. Perhaps the greatest risk is that something may happen to break or mar the glorious traditions of the past. I, on my part, will do everything possible to guard against such an occurrence, but perhaps I should point out that the future of this Lodge mainly rests upon those who will come after. They will be those that we, the present members, introduce. Let us, therefore, do as those who have gone before have done, viz., guard our portals with due care. No man should be proposed as a member of this Lodge unless we have very sound reason to believe he will be a worthy member of it. Let us strive to maintain the true family spirit within the Lodge, as by that means it can continue to be that haven of rest from the strife of the outside world which we have always found it. Most of you at some time when worried or depressed have found peace and communed with that indefinable something which gives peace, by walking along the sea shore, through the leafy lane, or over the open moor. That is how I have felt concerning our Lodge meetings, and may that feeling which I know has benefited others besides myself, long continue to exist, until time shall be no more."

According to the number of meetings in a year, so will be the number of times the Worshipful Master has to reply to the toast of his health, and at the least it may be said he

will have to do it four times. On the first occasion he may
well content himself by modestly acknowledging the honour
conferred upon him, and express his gratitude to the
Installing Master for the way the ceremony of his installation
into the chair was carried out. He need not, however, be
unduly diffident over his own capabilities. After all, the
brethren of the Lodge have shown their confidence in him
by electing him, therefore why attempt to prove them
wrong by displaying lack of confidence ? Reasonable
modesty is one thing, false modesty quite another. He can
conclude his speech on the installation night by going
straight on to propose the toast of the I.P.M. or of the
Installing Master.

On the second occasion he can refer to any special plans
or ideas he may have for his year, or refer to the particular
Institution, i.e., * R.M.I.G., R.M.I.B., R.M.B.I. or the
R.M.Hospital for the support of which he intends to take
up a list. In doing this, it is well not to overlook the fact
that though he be appealing for one particular institution,
the others are doing equally good work, for example :—

(90) "Charity is a distinguishing characteristic of a Freemason's heart. Each of you have had your attention
forcibly drawn to that point. It is important, as provision
for those in need has been realised as a necessity of life
since the earliest days of the Speculative Craft. You will
find it mentioned in the first Book of Constitutions, and
even before that in the days of the Gilds, it was customary
to provide for the bodily needs of the travelling brother in
distress. Many, in fact, are the instruments which Freemasonry to-day maintains to provide for the needs of
brethren and their dependents, foremost among them being
the Benevolent Fund of Grand Lodge, The Royal Masonic

---

* Particulars of the work of these Institutions, their history and
explanation of their need for funds can be obtained from the respective
secretaries.

Institution for Girls, The Royal Masonic Institution for Boys, The Royal Masonic Benevolent Institution, The Royal Masonic Hospital, Benevolent Funds in connection with Provincial Grand Lodges, London Rank and Private Lodges. The first Institution was the R.M.I.G., founded in March 1728, largely owing to the efforts of Chevalier Bartholomew Ruspini, and was then known as the Royal Cumberland Freemasons' School. Twenty years later, viz., in 1798, the School for the Boys was inaugurated largely owing to the efforts of Bro. William Burwood. In 1835 Bro. Robert Crucifix, first made efforts to form a fund for an 'Asylum for Worthy and Decayed Freemasons,' which ultimately became the R.M.B.I. in 1850. The Royal Masonic Hospital was a much later venture, originated by members of the Malmesbury Lodge in general, and Bros. Percy Still and C. H. Thorpe in particular. The Grand Lodge Benevolent Fund was originally a Fund of Charity, planned by the Duke of Dalkeith in 1724, when he was Grand Master. The magnificent work which our Institutions perform cannot be maintained unless the brethren provide the wherewithal. In these days of difficulty, stress, and uncertainty, their need is greater than ever before, and fortunately, thanks to the generosity of the Craft as a whole, the election system has not been in operation for some years past. To-night, as Master, it is my privilege to appeal for your support for the ———— (here name the Institution and give further details). I invite you to give what you can comfortably afford, but without detriment to those near and dear to you."

He should also remember to take the opportunity of expressing his appreciation of the work of the Lodge of Instruction. He may point out that he realises that his is the duty of remembering that the Lodge must function as a complete entity, each member working for the good of all, and that his endeavour will be to avoid anything approaching tyrannical rule, but rather to obtain the ready co-operation of the officers and members by means of precept and example, and continuously working for the Craft.

On the last occasion he may justifiably refer to work that has been done during his year, and should pay due compliment to the work done by the Treasurer, Secretary, and the Officers, not forgetting that those who "wait" also serve, in other words the Stewards, especially in a large Lodge, make some sacrifice of their personal enjoyment of the after-Lodge proceedings for the benefit of the other brethren.

The speeches he makes on the interim occasions afford him an opportunity of introducing matter of general Masonic interest and instruction which he may have gained by reading books or Masonic journals. In the case of Lodges of twenty years' standing, or more, the Master might introduce the idea of referring to the Lodge in its earlier days by studying the minutes, which can, of course, be seen by him by arrangement with the Secretary. It quite often happens that after thirty or forty years have gone by the remembrance of the customs and ideas in connection with the Lodge in its early days has grown dim, and useful work can often be done by referring back to them. On the other hand, the Master can often, with effect, make some reference to the old-time customs of the Craft, for example :—

(91) "Looking back to the night when I was installed into the chair of this Lodge, an event which for me marked the attainment of the ambition of my Masonic life, I realise that time is on the wing, and my year of office is now half over. Nevertheless, I am possibly more fortunate than I should have been had I been a Master in the eighteenth century, i.e., in pre-Union days, when a Master was usually only elected for a period of six months. In those early days Lodge meetings were held once a week, and therefore the brethren met together more often than we do now. On

the other hand we have our L. of I. the value of which, not only as a means of learning the ritual, but as a means of getting to know one's fellow Masons better, I cannot emphasize too highly. The ceremony of installation was much more simple than it is now, but the Master was charged to preserve the 'cement' of the Lodge. That is the note on which I would conclude my reply to-night. The Lodge may be said to represent a number of bricks which form a wall, but to unite them together there must be cement, and I personally feel that it is the particular concern of the Master to see that the cement is preserved, and thereby the harmony of the Lodge ensured. We have for some — years past concluded the record of our meetings in the Lodge minutes by saying that the Lodge was closed in perfect harmony, and it will be my earnest endeavour to see that that record is continued during my year of office."

Often much can be learned from studying the speeches of others. The following is an excellent example, and is taken from a speech of the late Sir Edward Clarke, and reported in the *Masonic News*)—

(92) "In 1902 the Duke honoured me by conferring on me the rank of P.G.W. and I wore my purple clothing for the first time at a great gathering of Canadian Masons who entertained me at Toronto during a trip through Canada. In 1912 my friends at the City of London College did me the honour of founding a new Lodge, calling it the Sir Edward Clarke Lodge, 3601, and inviting me to be its first Master. I have done several things which I hope may cause my name to be remembered when my life's work here is ended ; perhaps the Sir Edward Clarke Lodge will be the most lasting of my memorials. For I cannot imagine any changes in the political or social condition of England which can weaken the strong hold which Freemasonry has upon our people. I trust no such changes may take place, for I look upon our Masonic Lodges as centres of a powerful

influence which is constantly having effect in purifying and upholding our national character.

"The work of Masonry is essentiously religious. Its teaching has indeed no relation to the doctrines which distinguish and divide the Churches, but it proclaims at every meeting its reverence for T.G.A.O.T.U. ; it sings His praises ; it invokes His blessing upon all its work ; it teaches in all its formularies the virtues of brotherly love, charity, and truth ; the solemn obligations by which its members are bound together are only special sections of the Divine law which bids us fear God and love our neighbours.

"I do not say that all Masons are good men, but no bad man can be a good Mason and he will soon leave off attending Masonic Lodges, for to the man who is dishonest or immoral, or covetous, or uncharitable in thought, or slanderous in speech, it must soon be intolerable to listen to the noble teaching of the Masonic ritual. A full clear note is sounded in every hymn and every response in which he joins and to his conscience there must come at one the bitter reproach of insincerity and falsehood."

16

ELECTION AND INSTALLATION OF MASTER

NOTE—*Most of the following speeches could, without trouble, be adapted for the purpose of proposing Toasts and Replies thereto.*

(93)   To the Master-Elect

"Bro. ————, It is my pleasant duty to inform you that you have been unanimously elected to be Master of this Lodge during the coming year. It is a mark of the confidence which the Brethren have in you and your ability to fill this responsible position with success and in the true spirit of the traditions of the Craft. In this confidence I am sure they are right. Your year of office will be no light one, and I wish to say now, on behalf of all of us, that you may rest assured that our support and co-operation will be yours wholeheartedly. Finally, I wish to offer you our hearty congratulations on your attainment of the highest office available in the Lodge."

(94) *Reply.*

"W.M. and Brethren, I am much touched by this mark of confidence in me on the part of the Brethren of this Lodge. I am not so sure that I feel the same confidence in myself, but of one thing I am sure—that all my efforts during my term of office as Master shall be directed to upholding the dignity, the traditions and the privileges of this Lodge and of the Craft generally. Your generous offer to help I accept with gratitude, knowing that it is made with sincerity and in the true Masonic spirit. I thank you all very sincerely."

(95)   Toast to the Master-Elect

"Bro. . . . The brethren of this Lodge having unanimously chosen you as Master of this Lodge for the ensuing year, it is my privilege to congratulate you, and my pleasure to think that in a short while I shall have the pleasure of installing a brother and a friend, whom I got to know in the Craft. Your success as Master, as you are doubtless aware, will not merely depend upon performance of the ritual. In that regard you have well displayed your ability in the L. of I., but it will also be your duty to communicate happiness to and foster happiness among the brethren of this Lodge. Help will be yours for the asking. The past masters and those three stalwarts, the D. of C., the Treasurer, and the Secretary are always willing to render aid when properly called upon. To attain the chair, via the unanimous vote of the brethren is no mean honour, and one which I am sure you will value, not only this evening, but in the future. May your health be good, and your year a very happy one."

(96) *Reply.*

"Brethren . . . I have already expressed my thanks to you, and my appreciation of your confidence in me, in the Lodge. It is now many years, in fact . . . years to be precise, since I first saw Masonic light. Then, the view was expressed that I might one day attain the dignity of becoming Master of the Lodge. It seemed to be a far-off possibility—almost a dream. Now the time has come, but thanks to the helpful co-operation I have received from fellow members of the Lodge, I am approaching my new position of responsibility with some confidence, and will do my best to see that my work is performed with that sincerity which has been a distinguishing feature of this Lodge for many years past. I shall of course need your support, and feel confident that I shall receive it. I feel, however, that nothing can harm our Lodge or our Order, provided we as

Masons remember that our object is to give and not to get, and that we adhere firmly to our fundamental principle of service and goodwill."

(97)   TRANSFER OF HALL STONE LODGE JEWEL

It is suggested that this should be done at the close of the Installation of the new Master, immediately after the presentation of the Bye-laws.

"Finally, W.M., I entrust to your care the Hall Stone Jewel and Collarette of this Lodge, which as you know, was presented in Grand Lodge to a predecessor, as the representative of the Lodge in commemoration of the support given by its members collectively to the Masonic Peace Memorial. I therefore (present to, or invest you with) the Jewel, which should be worn by you on all Masonic occasions during your term of office as Master, and at the Installation of your successor be transferred to him.   Thus there will be continuous reminder to the Brethren now and in the future of the share taken by the Lodge in the great work, from which those who come after us may share in the advantages of the great Masonic Home now erected for the benefit and advantage of the whole English Craft."

(98)   VALEDICTORY ADDRESS BY W.M.

"Brethren, The period is rapidly approaching when the election of my successor will take place (or when my successor will be installed in my stead), and I take this opportunity of offering you all my cordial thanks for the fraternal kindness and support I have received at all hands, which has rendered my term not one of labour and dull routine, but one of pleasure, and I hope, advantage, to the Lodge.   (Short statement might follow of the work done, special functions, benevolence, and other circumstances). In these and all respects I have had the unfailing help of my Wardens and all the Officers of the Lodge, and, not least, consideration and accord of the whole of the Brethren.

I trust now that the service I have rendered has been apparent, you will realise I have served you to the best of my ability, and in all cases acted with judgment and reason. That I have endeavoured to carry out all my promises, that you have had your expectations realised, and that I have maintained the traditions of the Lodge, it is for you to decide, but I shall leave the Chair with the confident hope that I have met with your approval and in the full expectation of continuing to serve you in every way possible in the future."

(99)   MASTER'S ADDRESS AFTER INSTALLATION [1]

"Brethren, The conclusion of our ceremonies has now arrived, and I am regularly and legally, from the Masonic point of view, the Master of the Lodge. In me are vested powers and duties, and the obligation to maintain and support our ancient charges and regulations. In all the aspects of the Mastership I shall endeavour to act impartially with propriety of aim and fraternal regard for you all. I shall need your support, forbearance and consideration. From your generous nature and love of the Craft, I feel assured these will be mine in fullest measure. Whatever may be my failings or shortcomings, I look forward to the time when my willing service will be regarded with your approval and favour. I thank you all."

(100)   MASTER'S ADDRESS AFTER INSTALLATION [2]

"Brethren, you have now bestowed upon me the highest mark of appreciation which can be given by the Lodge : I trust that I shall continue to deserve your approval during my year of office as Master and afterwards. My duties are many and it is not the least of them to preserve the ancient charges and regulations of the Craft."

(If the M.E. has already been installed, it would be well to refer to his previous service in the Chair and alter the language accordingly.)

(101)   To an Installing Master
                        (not the I.P.M.)

"Brethren, One of the pleasant memories I shall ever
retain of our ceremonies to-day will be the fact that Bro.
———— performed the essential part of my Installation as
your Master.   Our long-standing friendship (or, my relation-
ship to him, he being, etc.) made it peculiarly gratifying
that he should have so taken part.   For his self-denial in
permitting this I give my personal thanks to our Bro. I.P.M.
To you, Bro. ———— as Installing Master, I need say no
more than I am very grateful to you, and the very dignified
and impressive manner in which you performed the ceremony
produced a strong and abiding effect upon me as, I believe,
it did on those who witnessed it.   You have thereby further
cemented our already strong personal relations and regard,
and adorned the ceremony by your sincerity and charm.
I thank you with all my heart."

(102) *Reply*.

"W.M., The privilege and pleasure so readily accorded
to me of taking the chief part in your Installation are themselves my reward.   Truly, I desired no reward, for our
friendship and associations are so firmly compacted that
nothing could be desired which we each would not do for
the other.   It is by such actions as those displayed by Bro.
I.P.M. that the amenities of the Craft are engendered and
amplified.   To him and all the Brethren I am deeply
indebted.   To you, W.M., I offer, with my thanks for your
remarks, my fervent wishes for a happy, constructive and
useful year of office, and thereby the increase in the cordial
relations existing between members of the Lodge."

The Immediate Past Master

On Installation Night it will be the duty of the new
Master to propose the health of his predecessor, the I.P.M.
This provides him with a useful opportunity of expressing

the thanks of the brethren for the services rendered during
the preceding year. If the I.P.M. also acted as Installing
Master, reference should be made to his work in that
connection.

General Ideas.

Appreciation of work done—Emphasise outstanding
points of the past year—Pay tribute to zeal displayed—
Emphasise possibilities for further work in the future.

(103)   TOAST OF THE IMMEDIATE PAST MASTER [1]

"On behalf of the brethren of the Lodge I have already
had the privilege and pleasure of presenting you with a
P.M. Jewel, and of tendering you their sincere thanks for
your efforts on behalf of the Lodge and the Craft during
the past year. This Lodge has been fortunate in having a
long chain of worthy brethren to fill the office of Master,
and you have proved yourself a very worthy link in that
honourable chain. The jewel which has been presented to
you is a mark of love, respect, and esteem, and your badge
as a Past Master ; it contains a representation of the diagram
for the 47th Proposition of the First Book of Euclid. You
possibly have some unhappy recollection of Euclid from
your school days, but I hope that naught but happy ones
will be associated with this jewel. Geometry, as you know,
is the fifth of the seven liberal arts and sciences, and the
particular proposition of Euclid referred to, proved that the
square on the hypotenuse of a right-angled triangle was
equal to the sum of the squares on the other two sides. It
enabled a square, as used by the operatives, i.e., an angle of
ninety degrees, to be obtained without the use of compasses,
because by setting out a triangle having sides of 3, 4, and 5
units respectively, an angle of ninety degrees could be
obtained. The design has considerable Masonic significance ; the large square, e.g., may represent the Master,
the two smaller ones the two Wardens. The triangle, the
strongest structure known to science, may signify the

strength of the G.A.O.T.U. while its three sides can also be considered to represent the three degrees, E.A., F.C., M.M. The right angle symbolically teaches the speculative Mason the necessity for upright conduct, and a due blending of our earthly and spiritual natures, and points out that only by square conduct, level steps, and upright intentions, can Masons hope to perfect themselves sufficiently and thereby become worthy to be numbered among the rulers in the Craft. May your jewel serve both as a memento of your year of office, and as a reminder of the purport of Masonry, and may you live long to wear it and to sojourn happily amongst us."

(104)   TOAST OF THE IMMEDIATE PAST MASTER [2]

"W. Bro. . . . it now falls to my happy lot to convey to you the warmest thanks of the brethren for your services during the past year as Master of this Lodge, and my own personal thanks for the impressive manner in which you installed me into the Chair of K.S. You can truly look back with pride and satisfaction upon a task well performed. As a tribute of regard of the brethren you have been given a P.M. Jewel, and you have been invested with the collar and jewel of a past master. Both bear a representation of the forty-seventh proposition of the first book of Euclid— the theorem of Pythagoras. The central feature is the right angled triangle, which is of special significance in Free-masonry, representing the strength of the Deity, and also the Triad. Its sides can be looked upon as representing the E.A., F.C. and M.M. The square on the longest side is equal to the sum of the squares on the other two sides. The larger represents the W.M., the two smaller the S.W. and J.W. respectively. Pythagoras discovered the relation-ships between the sides—the harmony of the square. The diagram in your jewel typifies the Craft, for is not a Masonic Lodge constituted of a number of men having possibly but one thing in common—a belief in a Supreme Being.

By our teachings and the application of the principle of brotherhood—the harmony of the square—we unite them into a harmonious body, not only within the Lodge, but within the Craft. Your jewel is therefore not only a mark of esteem, but also a symbol of brotherhood."

17

ADDRESSES AND TOASTS TO OFFICERS

Addresses to Officers (on investiture, where there is no usual formula, or it is not needful to use the full form, as in cases of long service).

NOTE—*Most of the following Speeches could, without trouble, be adapted for the purpose of proposing Toasts and Replies thereto.*

(105)   TO A CHAPLAIN

"Bro. ————, I appoint, etc., and invest, etc. The fact that you have (again) accepted this office is a source of gratification to the Brethren, and not less to myself. The nature of your duties is well known and it would be impertinent for me to detail them. The rendering of invocations and prayers here corresponds largely with your sacred duties elsewhere. (If the Chaplain is a layman, substitute, Your discreet and serious nature, and your elevation of thought and ideal eminently fit you for this office). We, therefore, rely not only on your decorous and seemly service, but on your advice and counsel on needful occasions, which your position and attainments well qualify you to give."

(106)   REPLY BY CHAPLAIN (WHEN ADAPTED
                 FOR USE AS A TOAST)

"W.M. and Brethren, For the cordiality with which you have proposed and received the Toast in my honour, I give you my grateful thanks. The W.M. appointed me to the position I occupy, and I am honoured by his action. That position has certain defined and limited duties, which, believe me, I will discharge to the best of my power. But

I regard myself as also charged with service to you on all occasions when, as an adviser and counsellor, I can assist in maintaining good feeling and unity, or increasing that fraternal affection and Brotherliness which are so eminently conspicuous in the Craft."

(107)   To a Treasurer

"Bro. —————, I invest you, etc. The Brethren, by their unanimous vote, have re-elected you Treasurer. This will be the ——th year of your service as such. We have had ample evidence of your knowledge of your duties, and your zeal and fidelity in the service of the Lodge, and it is not needful for me to say more than we are grateful for your continued service and care. The finances of the Lodge are in a very satisfactory state, and, while some of this is from causes over which you have no control, we know well that in the main it is the result of your watchful consideration and prudent management."

(108)   Reply by Treasurer (when used as
                    a Toast)

"W.M. and Brethren, I thank you for the recognition of my services by means of the Toast just given and received by the Brethren with every sign of accord and satisfaction. The duties of my office may at times require insistence on your attention, but I know that the demands of the Lodge will be met in the future with the same ready compliance as in the past. The work of a Treasurer is considerably lightened by such compliance and his office rendered less exacting. For this, and your present reception, I thank you most warmly."

(109)   To a Secretary

"Bro. —————, I appoint, etc., and invest, etc. For the last ————— years you have acted as Secretary of the Lodge, to the entire satisfaction of Masters and Brethren alike. Your knowledge of your duties and the details of the work entrusted to your care is, therefore, so ample that it is quite superfluous to recite to you the usual description. As in the past, we have had the benefit of your tact, toleration and assistance; we anticipate a continuance of your endeavours during the coming year. That our anticipations will be entirely realised, we are sure, and in return you may rely on our concurrence and co-operation, which will best illustrate our feelings of gratitude for all you have done, and will do, for the Lodge and the individual Brethren."

(110)   REPLY BY SECRETARY (WHEN USED AS A TOAST)

"W.M. and Brethren, The work of the Executive Officers of the Lodge is considerable, for they have to deal with many difficult problems, as well as matters of routine. I assure you that if at times you may not see eye to eye with us, it is not for want of desire on our part to serve or please you. The wide knowledge required to comply with the regulations and usages of the Craft at times precludes our acting otherwise, but we are certainly desirous of working for the good of all and the advantage of our Lodge. As the Secretary of the Lodge, I am actuated by this desire and am confident of your good feeling and kindness, which will enable me to carry out the work with that success which has just been emphasised by the proposal and reception of the Toast in so generous a manner. For all of these I offer you my sincere thanks."

(111)   TO THE TREASURER AND SECRETARY

"It has been said that every Lodge has two great pillars among the officers—the Treasurer and the Secretary. To the one we are indebted for the safe-keeping of our funds, and wise control over our expenditure. We may not always at the time welcome his admonitions to proceed cautiously lest our balance be adverse, but we know it is sound and given for our benefit. To the other we owe those impeccable records which are read in the form of minutes at every meeting. But we owe him more than that. He is the guide and counsellor of each succeeding Master, who should, but often does not know his Book of Constitutions in the manner that the Secretary does. It is customary in this Lodge to honour the invaluable services that these two brethren render the Lodge by giving them a special toast on Installation night, which toast I now ask you to honour."

(112)   To a Director of Ceremonies

"Bro. ————, I appoint, etc., and invest, etc. We have been fortunate in having had the benefit of your services in this office for several years, and have had experience of your skill and ability in all ceremonial matters, and the great knowledge you have of the work falling to your lot. We rejoice that you are willing to continue in office, for we know that under your direction and watchful care our ceremonies and all our doings will be carried on with dignity and decorum. Without your careful supervision we might degenerate into habits which would but ill-accord with the dignity and high importance of the Craft."

(113)   Reply by Director of Ceremonies
(when used as a Toast)

"W.M. and Brethren, The fraternal and complimentary remarks made in proposing the Toast, and your unqualified satisfaction in responding to it, are regarded by me as the expression of your approval of my work as D.C. In thanking you most heartily, I would remind you that much of my success has been the result of your willing submission and co-operation, and the help given by my A.D.C., for which I am grateful. My personal pleasure is consequently increased. That the direction of the ceremonies has received your approval increases my desire to be always at your service."

(114)   TO ASSISTANT OFFICERS [1]

"Bro. ————, I appoint you to be ———— and invest, etc. You will realise that the duties of any assistant call for considerable care and attention. It is not a formal or sinecure office to which you are appointed, but one where you can, and should, make it your charge to learn. The superior officer who is entitled to claim your help will, I am persuaded, give you instruction and advice, to which I ask your special attention, for by such means you will acquire knowledge to fit you for higher office and more particular service in the near future."

(115)   TO ASSISTANT OFFICERS [2]

"Bro. ————, I appoint you, etc., and invest, etc. In doing this, believe me, you are not to regard the office as of little account. A little help is worth more than a great deal of pity. That help you can, and must, give to Bro. ————, and we shall have feelings of pity for you should you fail to realise your opportunity and your responsibility. You are given this office to aid in forming your powers and acquiring the methods of serving the Lodge, and of the better qualifying you for greater service hereafter."

(116)   REPLY BY DEACONS (WHEN USED
                    AS A TOAST [1]

"W.M. and Brethren (on behalf of my Brother Deacon and myself), I thank you sincerely and cordially for the very kind way in which you have spoken of our work. Your approval is ample reward. I must say, however, that a large measure of such success as we have achieved is due to the whole-hearted co-operation and support of the other Officers concerned. This co-operation has eased our labour in the past—if I should call that a labour which gives so much pleasure in the doing—and adds greatly to the zest with which we look forward to our work in the future : I therefore take this opportunity of expressing publicly our gratitude to them. I can assure you that our services have always been, and will continue to be, at the disposal you have just expressed will make light the duties entrusted to us. We are deeply grateful to you."

(117)   REPLY BY DEACONS (WHEN USED
                    AS A TOAST [2]

"W.M. and Brethren, I am particularly pleased to have this opportunity of expressing thanks (on my own behalf, or for my Brother Deacon and myself) for the Toast just proposed and received in so generous a way. Your approval of our work as Deacons affords us much pleasure. That work, important and necessary as it is, can, we feel and know, only be effectively done with the aid of the other Officers concerned. By working together, as we do, our share is performed properly, and that it has your approval sets the seal on our efforts, which shall not be relaxed."

(118)   REPLY BY INNER GUARD (WHEN USED
                    AS A TOAST)

"W.M. and Brethren, It is indeed good of you to refer so generously to my work in the office to which you were good enough to appoint me. That office is not a sinecure, but it has been a source of pleasure to me, and I can honestly say that I have endeavoured to do my duty and to carry out efficiently the orders of my senior officer. Perhaps I may be pardoned, in view of the kind words used in proposing this toast and the reception which was given to it, for thinking that I have succeeded in winning your confidence and approval. I trust that I may continue to deserve them."

(119)   TO THE ALMONER

"Bro. ————, I appoint, etc., and invest, etc. In ancient times the care and distribution of alms and benevolent funds were entrusted to a man of settled character, charitable but firm in mind, and active in good works. You have already proved that those qualities animate you, and it is with satisfaction we shall rely on your advice and assistance in all cases of benevolence and the application of our contributions for that purpose. We know well that you will bring to your duties the tact, consideration and sympathy so needful to ensure that the recipient of our bounty realises the true import of Masonic brotherliness and affection."

(120)   TO THE ORGANIST

"Bro. ————, I appoint, etc., and invest, etc. Music, one of the seven Liberal Arts and Sciences which all Masons are exhorted to study, is well understood by you. There is little scope for exhibition of your instrumental powers in the course of our ceremonies, but appropriate and subdued music may relieve tedium and suspense. In the selection of the music to be performed, let me remind you that the most dignified and harmonious sounds proceed from the Common Chord based upon three notes. Let your services aid us to realise the three great principles on which the Order is founded, and find solace and satisfaction from your efforts."

(121)   TO STEWARDS

"Bro. ————, I appoint, etc., and invest, etc. The office to which you are appointed is both ancient and important. In former days the Steward was entrusted with many duties which are now performed by other Brethren, but there still remains some of the earliest with which the Steward was charged, namely, the care of the creature comforts of the Brethren, the entertainment of visitors, and a watchful interest in the limitation of needless indulgence and expense. Bro. ————, the senior among you is well qualified to direct and supervise your work, and we rely on your co-operation and interest."

(122)   REPLY BY A STEWARD (WHEN USED
                        AS A TOAST)

"W.M. and Brethren, my Brother Stewards and myself
are very gratified at the way in which you have expressed
your approval of our services. To adapt an old saying :
we can please some of the Brethren all the time, and we can
please all the Brethren some of the time, but we find it
difficult to please all the Brethren all the time. However,
we have done our best to accomplish even this difficult task,
and we hope we have had some measure of success—your
words, at least, lead us to think that we have. We trust
that our efforts in the future also will merit your approval."

(123)   THE TOAST OF THE WARDENS

"W.M. and Brethren, I feel greatly honoured in being
asked by the Worshipful Master to propose the toast of the
Wardens.

These Brethren have for several years been serving this
Lodge in various offices and they have done it admirably.
They are now within close reach of the Master's Chair and
we sincerely congratulate them. As they have progressed
year by year we have watched them with growing admiration,
not only because of what they are in themselves personally,
but because of the proficiency with which they have
invariably discharged their duties.

Masonry is one of those things which, if it fails to grip
and to call forth the full expression of its ideals in whole-
hearted and consecrated service, is certainly not achieving
its purpose. Our Wardens have won the esteem of the
entire membership of the Lodge by their efficiency and
devotion, and we are not only proud of them, but would
like them to know that they have won our esteem.

It is a wonderful experience for Brethren to feel the
bonds of brotherhood and spiritual fellowship uniting them
to one another in Masonry, to realise that though from time

to time one Brother after another passes out into the Unseen and Eternal, yet the work of Masonry goes on. Masonry is permament—not because of its ritual, its fellowship or its beneficence, but because it is built upon the ancient landmarks which are universally and eternally true. The greatest truths of Masonry are not its secrets but rather the things which are the common possession of all those Brethren who see life clearly and see it whole. In the consciousness of the tenets of Masonry, and in love and esteem for our Senior and Junior Wardens, I give you, Brethren, the toast of the Wardens."

(124)   REPLY BY A WARDEN (WHEN USED
                  AS A TOAST)

"W.M., In thanking you on behalf of my Bro. Warden and myself, as your Officers, I desire to say how gratified we are that you have selected us to aid in the ruling of the Lodge, and further to express to you our strong desire to serve you in every way consonant with our duties as Wardens and as Masons. We wish to co-operate with you and render you every assistance possible, and trust that our services will be approved by you and acceptable to the Lodge."

(125)   PROPOSAL OF TOAST BY A BROTHER

"Brethren, I am honoured by the command of the W.M. to propose the Toast of (name it). This honour I feel very diffident in accepting, but the knowledge of your sympathetic consideration for one who is endeavouring to cope with a difficult task, induces me to essay the duty entrusted to me. It does not need arguments to claim your approval of this Toast, for you realise that it is one which is particularly appropriate that we should show our approval of the work of the (object of Toast). Brethren, I claim your aid in honouring the Toast in a manner worthy of its nature and of your own generous dispositions as Brethren in the Craft."

(126)   REPLY BY AN OFFICER [1]

"W.M. and Brethren, For your very kind and generous words in proposing, and your ready acceptance of the Toast to (state purport), we, my colleagues and myself, offer you our best thanks. We take this opportunity of reiterating our full intention to perform our respective duties in the manner most to be desired—that is, to the extent of our ability. Whatsoever we may lack we shall endeavour to supply, so that we may receive from you at the close of our term of present office, an acknowledgment of your approval of our work."

(127)   REPLY BY AN OFFICER [2]

"Worshipful Master and Brethren, I appreciate very much indeed your very kind and generous words in proposing the toast of the Officers. On behalf of my colleagues and myself, I should like to offer you our best thanks. I take this opportunity of reiterating our full intention to perform our respective duties in the manner most to be desired, and should like to express appreciation of the confidence you have placed in them. On behalf of my brother Officers, I should like to assure the Master of our loyal co-operation during his year of office. Whenever greater calls may be made upon us we shall always be happy to give ready and willing service to you and the Lodge."

18

THE TYLER'S TOAST

THE Tyler's Toast is both a toast and a supplication, and should be delivered as such, leaving a due interval between the last words and the drinking of the Toast, for the real meaning to be impressed upon those present. The Tyler's office bears a symbolic meaning as does his sword which teaches us to set a watch at the entrance of our thoughts, place a guard at the door of our lips, and post a sentinel at the avenue of our actions. Bro. Tyler reminds us of our duties as a Freemason when we are about to enter the Lodge, and before we part at night his Toast reminds us of our sacred task to be mindful of the needs of others.

THE TYLERS TOAST.

All poor and distressed Masons, wherever dispersed over the face of Earth and Water, wishing them a speedy relief from all their sufferings, and a safe return to their native country, if they desire it.

19

THE INITIATE

THE toast of "The Initiate" provides the Master with a most valuable opportunity of following up the impressive work done in the Lodge. It should be regarded as a most serious effort and due preparation made. Well done, it can serve to impress the brethren present as well as the Initiate, and should be a distinct feature of the evening.

General Ideas.

Entered voluntarily—Ceremony only the beginning— Now one of a large family—Welcome to Lodge and Craft— Then of ideals expressed in the Charge—Need for discreet conduct becoming to a man—Practice the tenets both within and without the Lodge—Freemasonry a progressive science—Real advancement and understanding largely depends upon initiative and interest of the member.

(128)   TOAST OF THE INITIATE [1]

"I deem it not only a pleasure but a privilege to extend to you, Bro. . . . , a most cordial welcome both into this Lodge and membership of a Society which possesses a glorious past of which any Institution might be proud. Possibly your mind at this moment is not particularly clear concerning everything that you have heard and seen within the Lodge to-day, but as time passes, and you make, as I sincerely hope you will, a daily advancement in Masonic knowledge, the beauties of our ceremonies, and the tenets of the Craft will unfold themselves to you, and you will then the better appreciate the relative dependence of the several parts of our system of morality veiled in allegory, and illustrated by symbols. May I draw your attention to the pure white lambskin apron with which you were invested. The use of a white apron in connection with religious ceremonies dates back to the earliest times, when it was used as an emblem of purity, and of the ascent of the will over the lower or animal passions. It was also a token of sacrifice and a symbol of purification. It is of rectangular form, and when laid flat upon the ground might represent the plan or foundation site of a Temple or building, upon which you, as a Mason, have to erect a superstructure in the form of a personal character, perfect in its several parts, standing four square to all the elements, able to withstand the penetrating winds of malice, avarice, temptation and of vice. Whenever you wear it in the future, consider that in clothing yourself as a Mason you are performing a symbolic act, and are about to enter a Temple dedicated to the service of the Most High, and thus let it serve as a useful reminder of the duties you owe to your Creator, your neighbour, and yourself."

(129)   TOAST OF THE INITIATE [2]

"My first duty as Master of this Lodge is to extend to you a hearty welcome as a newly admitted member of the Craft and of this Lodge. While congratulating you on your admission as an E.A. it is also my duty to point out to you that you voluntarily sought admission into our Order. Someone well known to you, spoke in good report concerning your character. Had he not vouched for you, you could not have gained admission. You will, therefore, always be under a debt to your proposer to see that you do nothing to disgrace that apron with which you have to-day been invested. The important step you have taken to-day will probably open up to your eyes and mind, new ideas, greater vision, and I hope greater happiness in life, and a wider communion with your fellow men. You may think, or may hear it said, that you have been made a Mason. That is only partly true ; we have performed a ceremony by which you were admitted a member of our Ancient and Honourable Institution, but if you are to be a true Mason, the making must take place within yourself, and you, with our ready assistance, will materially contribute toward that moral and spiritual gain which can be derived from membership of the Order. As a child you were taught certain things at your mother's knee. To-day the importance of other things in life have been brought to your notice, and as you progress further in the Craft other great truths will be demonstrated to you. When the time comes for you to study our ritual, study it well, and you will find expressed in those beautiful phrases a system of morality veiled in allegory and illustrated by symbols. On the foundation laid this evening may you raise a superstructure honourable to yourself, which will reflect honour upon your proposer and credit to your Lodge. Ultimately by making a daily advancement in Masonic knowledge I hope you will reach the position I now hold, and in your turn endeavour as Master to impress others with the beauty, truth, and importance of our ceremonies."

(130)   TOAST OF THE INITIATE [3]

"Bro. Initiate, You are possibly aware that the ceremony of your initiation, although now completed, does not do more than originate the progress you hope, and we expect of you, in the Craft—that is, the Fraternity of Free and Accepted Masons. You have, indeed, but entered upon the preliminary stage of your Masonic career. You have seen the Masonic Light at its rising. Our ceremonies will increase both light and vision. Believe me, your future progress depends largely on yourself and your attitude to our Order. We have opened to you a new aspect of life and service ; you are one of a great Brotherhood, pledged to Love, Relief and Truth. Amongst Masons you will always be welcomed and at unison, so long as you comport yourself with due regard to the call the Craft makes upon you. It is a high, important and serious step you have taken, but amongst the family of Brothers into which you are now admitted you will find aid, counsel and support on the new road opened for your travel. Falter not, my Brother, but go forward seeking that which is high, noble and of good report.

You are placed to-night in the position of honour at my right hand, and we welcome you, we honour you for your aspirations, and you will honour us and the Lodge of which you are now a member by striving to attain the fullest knowledge, and utilising the great and invaluable privileges now within your reach. The day will come when your actions will be judged; may those actions be such that they will be found worthy of a great reward."

(131)   TOAST OF THE INITIATE [4]

"Bro. ————, you have been admitted to-night, a member of our ancient and honourable fraternity, and I should like to congratulate you on the step you have taken, and to express the hope that, having set your foot on the threshold of the Order, you will never turn back, but proceeding from strength to strength, will amply justify our judgment in accepting you as a candidate for initiation. I think it probable that your experiences to-night have been of such a nature that you are quite unable to form any useful opinion of Freemasonry. May I strongly recommend you not to attempt to do so, but I hope, and believe, those experiences will, on reflection, convince you that Masonry may, if you take advantage of the opportunities it offers, prove a great force for good in your life. I, as your W.M., confidently expect you to avail yourself of its teaching, and out of my own experience can promise you will receive a reward ; not a material reward but that indescribable emotion of pleasure and satisfaction that comes to those who, while cultivating the faculties the Great Architect of the Universe has given to them, find therein recreation in the highest sense of the word, rest and peace. I need hardly remind you that your *real* education, which commenced when you *left* school, is a slow process. When you set out in life and the world became your school-house, experience your teacher, work your syllabus, you entered on a curriculum that will extend to the last day of your life.

Do not, therefore, be discouraged if your Masonic education is also slow. Do not be discouraged if for a considerable period you apparently make but little progress. Be assured by me the Light is there, and as dawn follows night will gradually become visible to your understanding. Therefore set your face to the East, and let me advise you to take as your first subject for investigation, the *Study of Yourself*. Just quietly, fearlessly, and without favour, face *and* contemplate, your own character, and your own actions ; for when by means of that contemplation you arrive at a full consciousness of your insignificance in the presence of the great mysteries of Nature and Science, then, just then, you will have taken your first step on that road I will call progress, that leads to breadth of vision and greatness of character.

May I point out with, I hope, pardonable pride, you have been admitted a member of a very old Lodge, and one to which we, your brethren, think it an honour to belong. We, therefore, expect you to take particular care that no act of yours shall ever bring disgrace upon it. Be diligent in your attendance at our meetings ; obedient to those in authority ; courteous and helpful to the brethren on any and every occasion ; keen and anxious for the welfare and reputation of your Lodge ; and in two words, let me advise you to *walk humbly*, as a learner, in your Masonic career, for it is just those who do so the Brethren most delight to honour."

(132)   TOAST OF THE INITIATE [5]

"Bro. Initiate, you have taken a serious step in becoming one of the Fraternity of Free and Accepted Masons. You become entitled to many privileges, but you also assume great responsibilities. You probably do not yet realise the extent of either, but I may say that they will be in no way beyond what a man of upright and honourable character should expect. Your future career in the Craft will depend entirely upon yourself; if you would succeed, study deeply the principles upon which the Craft is founded and comport yourself according to them. The greater your experience in the Craft, the greater will be the pleasure and benefit you will derive from it. It is a great and honourable Brotherhood, and, if you live up to its ideals, there is no reason why you should not attain to high rank within it. Do not, however aspire to high rank for the sake of the rank alone, but for the opportunities which it gives of serving the causes which all of us have at heart and of forwarding the great ideal of universal Brotherhood. You will encounter difficulties on our way, but you will also receive willing help from those who have passed that way before you, and you will, in time, learn that Masonry is an ever-present help in time of trouble. I shall watch with great interest your progress along the Fraternal path, and I shall now ask the Brethren assembled here to wish you every success in the new life which you have commenced to-night."

(It is preferable that an Initiate should reply spontaneously. The sincerity of his intentions is then often more apparent than if he spoke by prompted words.)

(133)   TO A NEWLY-PASSED F.C.

"Bro. ————, You have this evening made a further advance in your Masonic life, and have become one of the ancient and honourable degree in the Craft. I believe and hope that the lessons of your Apprenticeship have sunk deeply into your mind and will animate your example and actions. In any case, keep them always before you for, although you are now able to do greater work, you have still much to learn and many difficulties to contend with.

Hence, you should keep your powers concentrated on your work—that is your life and actions. Let the roughnesses and irregularities be cleared away, and the symbol of your present Degree indicate your mental and spiritual state. To you this day has been indicated the nature of the further advance in knowledge expected of you. I earnestly commend this to you, for by such advance you will be fitted for greater service to your Fellows in the Craft, and the outside world."

(134) *Reply.*

"W.M. and Brethren, I am thankful beyond expression for your reception of me and my advancement to the degree of F.C. I feel more convinced than ever that Freemasonry is no thing of the moment, but contains the elements of constructive life and actions upon a basis, not yet, I fear, fully understood by me. For your counsel and advice I am grateful, and I look forward to your aid, and that of the Brethren, to enable me to become and remain one of your fellows in the work, and an ornament to the Lodge in whatsoever degree I may be."

(135)   To a Newly-raised M.M.

" Bro. —————, We congratulate you on having attained to the highest rank available to you in the Craft. It may not, and I trust will not, be the highest you will eventually attain, for you should aspire to become an Officer of the Lodge, and ultimately the Master and a Ruler in the Craft. To this end let me strongly urge you to continue, during the ensuing period, to leave no stone unturned in your search for Masonic knowledge. You are now expected to instruct and assist your Brethren less qualified than yourself, as was the case among our ancient Brethren. Therefore, you must increase your own knowledge and powers. Do not be content with the learning and memorising of our ceremonies, but strive always to understand and appreciate the meaning of those which are still veiled in allegory.

Above all, investigate and apply the principles and tenets, as well as the customs and usages, of our Craft, so that you may be amply qualified to discharge whatever Masonic duty may fall to your lot."

(136) *Reply*.

"W.M., To my indebtedness to you for the ceremony you have performed for my benefit and advancement, you have now added a further cause for my gratitude by your words of counsel and enlightenment. To express my gratitude fully is impossible in words, but I hope it will become apparent to you by my devotion and attention to the aims and purposes you have indicated. Should I become lax or inattentive, the Badge I now wear will be a perpetual reminder of my duty and a strong and lasting incentive to perform my task with zeal and fidelity. With all my heart I thank you and all the Brethren, and assure you of my intention and desire to do all in my power to be faithful to the trust reposed in me."

20

SOME OTHER SPEECHES

(137)   To a Brother Becoming Master of
Another Lodge

"Brethren, it is always a matter of congratulation when one of the members of our Lodge is installed in the Chair. If of our own Lodge, the pleasure is greater, because we have ourselves voluntarily and with due submission placed in his hands the power of ruling over us. But in any case we can, and do, share the pleasure of knowing that Bro. — — has been installed Master of the ———— Lodge, for thereby he has (become a Ruler in the Craft, and in case of emergency could act as Master here, or has added to his ruling powers and opportunities ; vary this as occasion requires). Bro. ————, we offer you our 'hearty good wishes.' It is an old formula of the Craft, but is expressive of our feelings and hopes for your year of office and its work."

(138) *Reply.*

"W.M., and Brethren, Your congratulations and good wishes inspire me, not only with pleasure but thanks and gratification. I have already appreciated the fact that there is a great advantage in the knowledge that in performance of one's duty, especially in Freemasonry, one has the confidence and the fraternal good wishes of one's Brethren. This is so even where the immediate duty is, as in my present situation, mainly to be performed in another place. The recollection of your kindness will be a strong aid and assistance to me, and the pleasure of your company in the —— Lodge will always be welcomed, not only by myself, but by all the Brethren of that Lodge. I am hopeful of arranging a meeting at which you can all be present as a corporate representative body of this Lodge, for I am persuaded that greater fraternal intercourse will be of advantage to both Lodge and to the Craft itself."

(139)   AT A LODGE CELEBRATION

"Brethren, You are all cognisant of the fact that the special purpose of to-day's meeting of this Lodge is to mark the (twenty-fifth anniversary of the consecration of the Lodge, or the fiftieth, or other period, or whatever may be the object of the function). Such an occasion is one for gratification and provides for a retrospect and prospect. In the first place let me offer a cordial welcome to all our visitors, especially (name such as are most important, or notable). We rejoice in their presence, and are glad to have their support. Then, too, we must mention Bros. ───── (names and remarks as to status, i.e., Founders, first Initiate, or Joining Members, Senior P.M.s, or the like). It is to these and other Brethren that the satisfactory and prominent position of our Lodge is due. By way of Retrospect, let me (state shortly the history of our past, or refer to the Historical Notes placed in your hands, as the case may require). We have much to be thankful for to those who have preceded us and those who constitute the Lodge to-day. We needs must remember those who have passed into the Great Beyond and their services to, and labours for, the Lodge. With deep gratitude we remember and honour them.

Then, Brethren, what of the Prospect ? The lessons of the past are needful to guide our future actions, but it is not well to be always looking back. Let us look forward with hope and desire, for the Future does not exist except in To-day. We have to our hands a potent organisation for the good of the Craft and the advantage of Humanity. There will be presented to us in never-ceasing succession opportunities for the exposition and practice of the great ideals, principles and tenets of our profession, for the pursuit of pure and unselfish aims, the relief of the distressed, sad and needy, the extension of unity and cohesion in the Craft Universal, and the maintenance and furtherance of our own fraternal relations. Let the example of our predecessors and the spirit of the Past, as well as of the everpresent Future, animate us to the most complete, abounding service and to the building up of the great and glorious heritage we have received into a more bright and beautiful possession to be transmitted pure and unsullied to those who come after us. May this Lodge flourish and increase until time shall be no more."

(Special care must be taken to adjust the foregoing to the particular circumstances and event.)

(140) Visit of Provincial Grand Lodge

"R.W.Prov. G.M., and Brethren. As the W.M. of the ———— Lodge, I offer you the cordial welcome of the Lodge, and express our sincere gratitude that the Prov. G.L. of ———— (has held, or is to hold) its meeting under our Banner. We sincerely trust that the arrangements we have made for the accommodation, comfort, and, may I add, the entertainment of the Prov. G.L., and the Brethren will meet with your approval. We rejoice that you are present with us on this occasion, for we are assured that such an event will do much to increase the unity of the Lodges in the Province and link the Brethren together in closer harmony. The wide extent of the Province will thus become of no real moment. The cause of charity, too, will, we believe, be regarded with greater desire to improve upon the already good results achieved. As the needs of Lodges in the Province become more widely known and understood, a greater and more sympathetic feeling will ensue. On the other hand, the claims of the Province will be responded to with fervour and self-sacrifice. To you, personally, R.W.Prov.G.M., we offer our felicitations and our good wishes for your health and strength to be maintained, so that your beneficent rule may continue for many years to come."

(141)   ABSENT BRETHREN

"Brethren, In times past the custom arose for Freemasons in their Lodges to remember their Absent Brethren, and the terms of what is now the Tyler's Toast were compiled to effect this remembrance so far as Brethren in need were concerned. As that Toast does not include those Brethren who are absent from other causes, my predecessors maintained a Toast on the subject, as you know full well. Let me remind you specially of (name any Brother specially to be remembered and circumstances of absence). We know that at this time our absent Brethren are thinking of the observance of this custom and are in unison of spirit with us. We wish them all good, and hope the time will shortly come when they can once more be in our company."

(The Toast "Absent Brethren" given with usual honours.)

(142)   A LODGE TOAST

"Brethren, It seems to me appropriate, and not objectionable, that we should on certain occasions, such as the Installation Meeting, express our sentiments towards the Lodge as a community or corporate body. It is true that this is like complimenting ourselves, but only so if we regard the Lodge as being only the aggregation of its members. Considered as the meeting itself, one might still say it is ourselves we honour, and in this case it would not be amiss to do so. But I want you to realise that the Lodge is an entity apart from ourselves, an organism intangible but none the less real, an object of affection and regard quite apart from our mere membership. It is like the Home, more than a residence, or place for gathering together. We are proud of our Mother Lodge, and hold it in reverence as if it were our parent.   In this aspect let me commend to you with all sincerity and enthusiasm the Toast of 'Our Lodge'."

(The foregoing could be adapted to a School or Professional Lodge under its special title.)

21

BENEVOLENCE AND CHARITY

(143)   FOR A MASONIC INSTITUTION

"Brethren, It is often said that the value and importance
of our Craft is shown in its support to the three great
Institutions we have existing for the aid and assistance of
Girls, Boys and Old People, as we affectionately say. This
is, in part, true, but it is not the sole purpose for which
our Craft exists. We, like practically all Lodges, have our
own Benevolent Fund, from which some help is given to
the funds of the Institutions, but primarily the Lodge Fund
is devoted to the aid of distressed Brethren and their
dependants, as well as to other charitable causes or objects.
Limiting my remarks to the particular cause I desire to
advocate, I may remind you that I am representing this
Lodge at the next Festival, to be held in ——— next, of the
Royal Masonic ——— (name Institution). I earnestly
invite your support to as full an extent as prudence and the
Masonic principle permits. I hope your response will be
spontaneous and generous, and that the result will be a source
of satisfaction that the Lodge has done well and worthily
in the cause of Charity."

The reply may be by the Secretary of the Institution, if
present, or by the Almoner, or Charity Representative, or
a Brother who can give particulars and details of the needs
to be met.

(144)   FOR THE ROYAL MASONIC HOSPITAL

"Brethren, The cause I have to bring before you is one
which I feel confident will appeal to you with force and
evoke your sympathy. In our three great institutions we
provide for those who are in need but are otherwise in

health and strength, and so far as may be are not sick or suffering. It was a truly Masonic feeling which considered the need for a Freemasons' Hospital and Nursing Home, where our Brethren or members of their family could be under the best medical, surgical and nursing care possible, within reasonable cost, and surroundings of a Masonic nature. The Hospital has nobly fulfilled its task, but the claims upon it increase daily, not only by applicants in London, but from Provinces near and far, and from Overseas. The work still increases, and more accommodation is needed and extension of the buildings a paramount necessity. This Lodge has assisted with donations in the past (if a Founding Lodge, so state), but as the claims increase we ought to take our share in meeting them. I therefore, appeal to you to place on the list your name, and state the amount you are prepared to give, which in due time will be collected by the Almoner. Brethren, I will leave the subject to your generous instincts and personal feeling."

(145)   FOR THE SAMARITAN FUND

"Brethren, You are aware that it is the custom of this Lodge to devote once a year the contents of our Charity Box, which will shortly be brought round to you by Bro. Almoner, to the Samaritan Fund. I would remind you that the Fund was originated to aid Brethren and their dependants who were not in a financial position to discharge the actually low fees and expenses of their treatment, and for similar purposes. The number of calls upon the Fund are many and increasing. Here is an opportunity for showing true kindness and mercy. Brethren, take it and let our yearly contribution be an indication of your desire to aid the afflicted and needy."

(146)   ON A CLAIM ON THE LODGE
                    BENEVOLENT FUND

"W.M. and Brethren, It is needful under our regulations
that the Lodge should authorise a special expenditure out
of our Benevolent Fund for any purpose for which the
Fund is applicable. The truest form in which we can be
benevolent is to leave the investigation of the case of any
applicant to the Committee of the Fund, on whose behalf
I am authorised to say that they are abundantly satisfied of
the propriety of assisting a Brother (or a widow of a Brother)
who is in dire need of help. We, therefore, ask you to vote
a sum of £——— to be applied by the Committee or
myself as the Almoner of the Lodge, in the relief of the
claimant to the best advantage."

If a petition to the Grand Lodge Fund of Benevolence is
to be presented, the circumstances should be stated and the
needful procedure followed.

(147)   FOR A PROVINCIAL BENEVOLENT FUND

"Brethren (if by W.M. ; or if by another Brother, W.M.
and Brethren), You are aware that in this Province there
has been established for a long time a Benevolent Fund to
deal with the needs of local Brethren, their widows and
orphans. This supplements the benevolence of the various
Lodges constituting the Province, and is in no way detri-
mental to our efforts for the great Masonic Benevolent
Institutions, which we support in no niggardly manner.
Indeed, our Provincial Fund often renders unnecessary
many appeals to the Fund of Benevolence of the Craft and
aids in no uncertain way to minimise claims on the Institutions. I am particularly anxious to bespeak your generous
support for our own Fund at this time, for the particulars

of its work, which are before you, will amply demonstrate its value, and its needs, as you will see, are urgently pressing. I assure you, whatever aid you can give will be thankfully received and faithfully applied."

22

SOCIAL FUNCTIONS

Note—It is suggested that no Masonic practices or terms should be used. At most the title Brother ought to suffice. Toast should be given without accompaniment of any kind.

Ladies' Festival

Loyal Toast, "The Queen", given without comment.

(148)   To the Ladies [1]

"Brother President, Gentlemen and Brethren, It has fallen to me to propose what may be regarded as the most popular toast of the evening. Realising this, I confess that I begin to quail before the responsibility which rests upon me. We look forward to this annual Festival because it is a means of doing honour, and, we hope, of giving pleasure to our lady friends and relatives. Ladies, do not judge our ordinary work by what you see to-night. But let me assure you that we look forward so long and so joyously to this Festival which allows us an opportunity of fulfilling certain social duties. What I do wish to say is, 'Ladies, you are right welcome.' The words are old but they express true spirit of British hospitality. We trust that you will enjoy the evening thoroughly, and that your recollections of a Masonic Ladies' Festival will be of the happiest and pleasantest. Brother President, Gentlemen and Brethren, I ask you now to charge your glasses and to drink to the health of 'The Ladies'."

(149)   To the Ladies [2]

"Bro. President, In discharging the duty laid upon me of proposing the Toast of 'The Ladies,' I am sure you and the Gentlemen and Brethren present will acquit me of

fulsome flattery when I say how delighted we are to have the
company of so many Ladies.   Their presence and gracious
condescendence adds to our pleasure and creates a feeling
of happiness and gladness.   Our Festival is designed to
please the Ladies and to make them feel that our endeavours
are not selfish.   We have so far experienced every satisfaction, and for the remainder of the evening the programme
laid down offers every possibility of that satisfaction being
maintained.   Ladies, we are delighted to see you, proud to
be in your company, and we hope the evening will prove a
Festival in the highest sense."

(No reply is suggested here for a Lady or a non-Mason,
but if a Brother replies, the following may suffice.)

(150)   *Reply.*

"Bro. President, in the unaccountable circumstance of no
Lady being willing to speak in reply to the Toast, I have
been selected to do so on their behalf.   I do not exactly
know what are the feelings of the Ladies following the
remarks of the proposer of the Toast and the exhilarating
manner it was received by the male members of the company,
but I feel sure their feelings, being too deep for words, are
of the most appreciative and pleasurable character.   That
being so, I offer you the sincere thanks of the Ladies for
all you have done, are doing, and will do, to ensure their
happiness and pleasure during the Festival."

(151)   ON PRESENTATION TO LADY

"Madam, I am charged by the members of the Lodge,
of which your husband, our Bro. President of this evening,
is the Master, to offer for your acceptance a small token for
your personal use, as a memento of this evening's proceedings, which we are happy to feel are graced by your presence,
and also as some indication of our esteem and regard for
our Brother, and appreciation of all he has done as Master.

We invite your acceptance of the gift, in the hope it will be a constant reminder of our gratitude to you and him."

(152)   OUR GUESTS [1]

"Gentlemen and Brethren, I propose only addressing those who are members of the Lodge, for the Toast I now wish to submit is that of 'Our Guests,' not meaning thereby, I regret to say, the Ladies, because they have already been honoured, as it should rightly be, seeing that Toasts originated as a compliment to Ladies.   Now it is not a question of merely offering our hospitality to the gentlemen and Brethren who are our guests this evening, but we desire to show them how welcome they are, and how truly pleased we are that they have been able to take part in this Festival. To our Masonic Brethren it is needless to emphasise this. To those gentlemen who are not Masons, we say that we entertain for them the highest opinion and assure them that their presence is appreciated, and we sincerely hope that, in other circumstances, or at some future time, we shall be again honoured by their sharing in our Festival and adding to our pleasure."

(153)   OUR GUESTS [2]

"Gentlemen and Brethren, It is needless for me to point out that there is a distinction between the two terms I have used, but no difference in our estimation of the pleasure our guests have given to us by their presence to-night.   Let me say without offence that while Gentlemen may not be as much to us as Brethren, yet Brethren are Gentlemen, with the added tie which Masonry confers upon its members. You are all equally welcome, equally held in honour, and equally entitled to our regard.   You have, we hope, enjoyed the Festival so far, and will, no doubt, be entertained still further.   We offer you all our very best wishes and congratulations."

(154) *Reply*.

(No reply is given for a non-Mason, but only for a Brother.)

"Bro. President, Ladies, Gentlemen and Brethren, It would indeed be a want of courtesy and propriety did I not at once assure you on behalf of all the guests who are Masons, of our pleasure at being given the privilege of attending this Festival, and of thanking you in all sincerity for your welcome, and the boundless care and attention bestowed on us, from which we have experienced the greatest pleasure. Our admiration and interest are very vivid, and the presence of so many ladies has made the evening most happy and delightful. We know the secret of Masonic hospitality, we have experienced it to the utmost, and we one and all are grateful."

(155)   To the President

"Ladies, Gentlemen and Brethren (if by a non-Mason, omit the 'Brethren'), The success of any meeting, large in numbers, especially as this is, depends almost entirely on the tact, affability and courtesy of the Ruler of the Feast. It was so of old, and is so now. We know full well how much care and attention has been exercised by Bro. President to ensure the comfort and entertainment of each one of us. His kindly and thoughtful attention has not flagged, but in every respect he has fully maintained our interest and been a powerful factor in our pleasure. To evince your accord with these remarks, I ask you all to join with me in drinking the Toast of 'Our President'."

(Given without accompaniment, or cheers, or "Jolly Good Fellow", which detract from the dignity and propriety of the occasion.)

(156) *Reply*.

"Bro. ————, I am conscious of many defects, and possibly neglect of opportunities which to myself I lay to

my charge. The remarks made in proposing the Toast in
my honour, and the cordial reception you have given to it
assure me, however, that you have not suffered from any
default of mine. To me the occasion is one for satisfaction
and congratulation, for you have all been so obviously
happy that I congratulate myself in having the honour of
presiding over this Festival. I give you my best thanks.
But I must not, and do not, claim the credit for this evening's
pleasure for myself alone. The Committee charged with
the arrangements have carried out all the details with energy
and foresight. To them our combined thanks are due, and
notably to Bro. ————, who is the Secretary of the Committee, and has done yeoman service on our behalf.   I
therefore invite you to show your thanks by honouring the
Toast of 'The Committee'."

(157) *Reply*.

"Bro. President, Ladies, Gentlemen and Brethren, On
behalf of the Committee, I return you our sincere thanks.
We have worked with a single eye to your pleasure, and
rejoice to know our work has not been in vain. The knowledge that you are pleased and satisfied is our reward. You
look forward to the remainder of the evening, free from
speeches, but replete with opportunity for social harmony
and pleasurable incidents. It is our desire that your wishes
should be fulfilled and the measure of your happiness will
be the measure of our own."

23

OTHER FUNCTIONS

(158)   To a Visiting Team

"Brethren, The association of the particular sport we favour with Masonry is particularly happy in its results. To contest in friendly rivalry in a form of sport which in itself is without reproach will undoubtedly be of great value in forming our powers of endurance, of friendly consideration, and of emulating the Brotherliness which is one of the great principles of our Craft. To strive mightily, without asperity, to lose gracefully, and to win without boastfulness, are results we have gained, or shall gain, from our contest, and I can only add that it is in the spirit I have indicated that all these meetings can, and will, be conducted, and all will be pleased in the knowledge that the best team will win (or has won)."

(159)   Thanks to a Lecturer

"Bro. ————, We unite in offering to you our sincere thanks for your presence here this evening and for your most interesting and instructive lecture on (state subject). We have received much enlightenment from your lucid exposition of the subject dealt with, and your remarks and information have opened to us new avenues for thought and enquiry. We feel it is by such means we can not only do honour to you, but emulate your example, and increase our knowledge and understanding of our great Fraternity, its history, the symbolism and hidden meaning of our ceremonies, and the greater appreciation of the ideals, principles and tenets of our profession. We give you our grateful thanks in full and ample measure."

(If a resolution is needed, it should be moved and carried.)

(160) *Reply*.

"W.M. and Brethren, I am impressed by the sincerity of
the remarks you have made, the cordiality of my reception
(and the terms of the resolution you have adopted).   The
attention and interest displayed by you all in my address
have satisfied me that you are determined to carry out the
injunction laid on us all, to make a 'daily advancement in
Masonic knowledge'.   That I have been able to assist you
in this, is a great pleasure to me, and your kindness and
fraternal welcome my sufficient reward."

(161)   To Brethren Giving a Demonstration

"Brethren, We have the pleasure of receiving this evening
a number of Brethren representing the (state nature of
object of visit, and names and rank of those taking part).
I am well aware that by giving their demonstration every
attention, we shall derive from it much knowledge and
information.   I need do no more now than to bespeak your
consideration of and interest in the proceedings.   I will,
therefore, ask our Brethren to undertake their task."

(After the demonstration, it would be well to have a
formal resolution passed, to be entered on the minutes.)

(162)   Thanks to those Brethren

"Brethren (or W.M. and Brethren, if given by a Brother
other than the Master).   At the close of this most interesting
demonstration there is for us the pleasurable duty of
expressing our unbounded thanks to Bro. ———— and his
colleagues for the splendid service they have done us, and,
incidentally, to the Craft, by their exposition of (describe
nature and any special matter of interest).   To us this
demonstration has been of great value and instruction. One
cannot fail to realise how much united teamwork is necessary
to fully express the full meaning and beauty of the work.
This is a great lesson for all of us.   Too often the ceremonial
work of our Lodges suffers from want of combination and

co-operation among those who take part, although in many cases the work of individuals is of the best. Let us lay this to heart and profit by the exposition we have witnessed. The sincerity, finish and method just exhibited are testimony to the skill and understanding of all who have taken part. Nothing further is wanted to enable us to offer the Brethren our most grateful thanks for their services, and their example of how we too should act. We thank them all without exception, and shall long remember this evening's ceremony with pleasure."

(Resolution of thanks.)

(163)　　REPLY (BY THE LEADER OR DIRECTOR OF THE WORK)

"W.M. and Brethren, On behalf of my colleagues and myself, I tender you our heartfelt thanks for your reception, and the interest you have taken in our demonstration. (Some remarks as to its special import, or as may be, could be here interpolated.) I assure you, Brethren, it has been a special pleasure to us to be here, and that you have been interested we feel sure, from your sympathetic following of our words and actions. If our work has not only interested you, but has stimulated you to further enquiry, or may be of assistance to you in the future, we shall feel well repaid. For the rest, W.M. and Brethren, pray accept our most grateful thanks and compliments."

24

THE ROYAL ARCH

The speeches which may be needed can be easily adapted from those already given. It should be carefully noted that the needful and proper changes of address, titles, and so on, should be made.

(164) TO THE PRINCIPALS OF THE CHAPTER

"Your Excellencies, The duty, which is also an unfeigned pleasure, laid on the I.P.Z. of proposing the Toast of your health, is one which I discharge with every feeling of satisfaction. You fill a high and honourable office. Acting conjointly and at times separately, yet always in accord, you have held up to the Companions an example of dignity and service. The members of the Chapter have every confidence in your rule, and we are happy to think that your service to the Chapter will be productive of the highest results. To that end, our co-operation and support will be continuously and generously given."

(165) REPLY BY M.E.Z.

"Ex.Comp. ————, For your compliments and assurances of co-operation, we are extremely grateful. The spirit of fraternal companionship is so amply exemplified by all the Companions, and the assistance of every officer in his particular sphere is so freely and ungrudgingly accorded to us, that our labours are light and pleasant. We shall endeavour to the utmost of our power to carry out the traditions of the Chapter and to follow in the steps of our illustrious predecessors as long as we hold office, or are members of the Chapter."

(166) To a Principal (H. or J.)

Although the Toast usually is to the three Principals conjointly, occasions may occur when a separate Toast would be appropriate to one or both of the Principals.

"M.E. and Companions, I am charged with the pleasant duty and obvious privilege of proposing a Toast in honour of (the 2nd and 3rd Principals, or E.Comp. H., on his having been elected to the office of 1st Principal, or E.Comp.J., on his election as 2nd Principal, or as the case may require). We have observed with satisfaction the manner in which our E.Comp. has shared in the ceremonial and in the ruling of the Chapter. The earnest rendering of the work and the cordial manner exhibited at all times have led us to believe that in the future those qualities and powers we admire will be devoted to the best interests of the Chapter and the Companions without distinction of rank or position. All our confidence and appreciation will be justified by the results."

(167) Reply by H.

"M.E. and Companions, I thank E. Comp. ———— for the generous terms in which he submitted the Toast and your approval of it. It is a great delight to me that you have been satisfied with my actions (and that you have elected me to the 1st Principal's chair). I can honestly assure you that no endeavour on my part shall be wanting in the future to justify your confidence in me. The task may call for the utmost I can do to accomplish your desires, but with your fraternal and sympathetic support and good-will I trust that when the time comes for me to lay down my sceptre of immediate rule you will be able to say that I have served you well and faithfully."

(168)   REPLY BY J.

"M.E. and Comps., I am truly grateful to you all, and
more so to E.Comp. —————, for the Toast just given with
such fervour. I am conscious of many doubts, for the
future holds such opportunities requiring skill and ability,
with knowledge of our ceremonies, that I fear I may not
be able to properly and efficiently play my part. But let
me assure you that in the meantime I shall take every care
to qualify myself for the offices which I may yet have to fill.
The knowledge that you have approved of what I have done
thus far will inspire me to so acquit myself that I shall
follow in the steps of my illustrious predecessors, with
success and satisfaction to you all and myself."

(169)   TO AN EXALTEE

"Comp. Exaltee, We have already congratulated you
on having been exalted into this Sublime Degree. It forms
an integral part of 'pure and ancient Masonry' as defined
in our English Craft, and we are sure that a more full
acquaintance with our ceremonies than you have yet been
able to make, will convince you that this Degree or Order
is properly termed Sublime. The language, symbolism and
teaching of our ceremonials are both beautiful and profound.
Learn all you can of these, and let the truths we have unfolded
to you sink deeply into your mind and heart. Thus will
you justify your exaltation and prove that our confidence
in your intentions and desires has not been misplaced."

(170) *Reply.*

"M.E. and Companions, In the first place, I feel impelled
to say how much I value your words, M.E., and the
reception which has been accorded to me on my exaltation
and admission into the Chapter. During the interval since
the ceremony I have endeavoured to analyse my feelings
tonight with those of my initiation into the Craft. Then
I was filled with some wonderment and some surprise, but

with the realisation I had taken a serious step leading to a higher appreciation of my duty to my Fellows. To-night the beauty and depth of meaning in all I have seen and heard leave me unable to express all I would like to say. I think the ceremony is rightly called Exaltation, for the high tone and teaching exemplified are so exalted that one can only feel that the end is one to be sought in humility and dependence. My best endeavours will be constantly directed to the fullest understanding of the ceremonies and teaching. I crave your aid and offer my heartfelt thanks."

25

THE MARK DEGREE

The same remarks as above apply to speeches in this Degree, or its associated Degree. The modes of address, titles and Officers should be carefully noted, and the phrasing adapted as circumstances may require.

(171)   To the W.M.

"Brethren, The example set by our W.M. during his progress in this Degree, and during his present year of office, has been of the highest, and has inspired us with feelings of admiration for himself and of pride and pleasure to be under his rule. Above all, he has exemplified the beauties of this Degree and the importance of its principles in a manner which has convinced us that those Craftsmen who do not take this Degree are losing a vital and integral part of their Masonic life. To our W.M. I express, on your behalf, our thanks for, and appreciation of, his unfailing courtesy, high level of service and generous recognition of the aid given by the officers, and the sympathetic consideration of our shortcomings."

(Toast, if given, with appropriate accompaniment.)

(172) *Reply*.

"Bro. ————, if I were not certain that you would not adopt a tone of fulsome flattery to any one or myself, I should feel unduly elated by your remarks. I can, and will, only say that I thank you exceedingly for your approval of what I have done in the past. I shall endeavour to carry out in the future all my duties to your satisfaction, so that when you come to reckon with me you will be able to say I have made my mark upon our Lodge and on the hearts of the Brethren."

(173)   To an Advancee

"Bro. Advancee, We welcome you into this Ancient and Honourable Degree as well as to our Lodge. During your progress through the ceremony of Advancement you could not fail to realise the dignity and importance of it, or the great and abiding principles involved. It is, indeed, no empty ceremony, but contains, as you must have realised, much that is of enduring permanent value to you in your life and actions. The apparent failures of life may, and often do, become the triumph and success of well-spent time and energy. To you it is no vain or evanescent assurance that among Mark Masons you will ever find those ready to stand by, and assist, you in all the changes and chances of life, and while you remain faithful and worthy you will always be assured of the great reward of those who overcome. Strive on to fulfil your allotted task while it is yet day, for the night cometh when no man can work. If you endure to the end there will arise for you the brightness of the Eternal Day."

(174) *Reply.*

"W.M. and Brethren, I see in the grave but beautiful words you have addressed to me the assurance that in this Degree, with the initial ceremony of which I have been greatly impressed, I shall find much to consider and investigate. I am grateful to you for the welcome you have proffered, and I look forward to time well spent in the practise of this Degree. Your help and direction in my advance will be highly appreciated and valued by one who has yet much to learn but who is sincerely desirous of becoming a real Brother to you all."

26

MODES OF ADDRESS

THE foregoing pages will, it is hoped, have provided the Mason who desires to improve his capabilities as an after-dinner speaker with a general outline of how to proceed, and possibly have been of particular assistance to those about to go into the chair of a Lodge. It is, of course, impossible within the compass of a small volume to provide a complete course of instruction and to give alternative outline speeches for every occasion.

It will possibly have been noticed that in giving outline speeches, no opening phrase of address has been given. The author felt it would be better to set these out in the following tabular form, which provides the correct prefix for brethren of all ranks.

MODES OF ADDRESS

For opening a speech, or at other times as occasion requires, Iteration of Names, Titles or Office should be avoided as much as possible.

Special attention should be given to the Notes at the end and modes of address varied accordingly when needful.

THE CRAFT
GRAND OFFICERS

Grand Master *Pro Grand Master*	Most Worshipful
Deputy Grand Master *Assistant Grand Master* *Provincial Grand Master* *District Grand Master* *Grand Wardens*	Right Worshipful

Grand Chaplain
Grand Treasurer
Grand Registrar
Deputy Grand
  Registrar
President of Board of
  General Purposes
Grand Secretary
President of Board of
  Benevolence
Grand Director of
  Ceremonies
Grand Inspector
Order of Service to
  Masonry
	Very Worshipful

All other Grand Officers	Worshipful Brother

GENERALLY FOR ALL BRETHREN NOT OTHERWISE SPECIFIED

Grand Stewards being Installed Masters Masters of Lodges	Worshipful Brother
Master (in the Chair)	Worshipful Master
I.P.M.	Worshipful Brother Immediate Past Master

Past Masters, including
  London Grand Rank
  and Overseas Rank,
  in office or not
	Worshipful Brother

Brethren of and below the degree of M.M.	Brother

PROVINCIAL GRAND OFFICERS

Provincial G.M.	Right Worshipful Provincial Grand Master
Deputy Prov. G.M.	Worshipful Bro. Deputy Prov. G.M.
Assistant Prov. G.M.	Worshipful Bro. Assistant Prov. G.M.
All other Provincial Grand Officers being Installed Masters	Worshipful Brother

DISTRICT GRAND OFFICERS

As for *Provincial Grand Officers*, substituting "District" for "Provincial".

THE ROYAL ARCH

The 1st Grand Principal	Most Excellent First Grand Principal
Pro 1st Grand Principal	Most Excellent Pro First Grand Principal
2nd Grand Principal	Most Excellent Second Grand Principal
3rd Grand Principal	Most Excellent Third Grand Principal
All other Officers of Supreme Grand Chapter	Excellent Companion
Principals of Chapters	Most Excellent First Principal Excellent Comp. 2nd Principal Excellent Comp. 3rd Principal

Past Principals in office or not }	Excellent Companion
Other Officers and Members }	Companion

THE MARK DEGREE

The Grand Master, Provincial Grand Master Deputy Grand Master Grand Wardens }	As in the Craft
President of the General Board }	Right Worshipful Brother
Grand Overseers „ *Chaplains* „ *Treasurer* „ *Registrar* „ *Secretary* „ *Dir. of Cers.* }	Very Worshipful Brother
Provincial (or District) Grand Masters {	Right Worshipful Provincial (or District) Grand Master
Deputy Prov. or Dist. G.M. *All other Grand Officers* }	Worshipful Brother
Masters of Lodges Masters in the Chair Past Master I.P.M. Brethren below the rank of Installed Master }	As in the Craft

NOTES.—Where no title or office is indicated, the name of the Brother with any distinction of position should be added as V.W.Bro. Sir, ... In some circumstances the office held by the Brother addressed should be added also, as where the particular office is being referred to.

The addresses given throughout apply to actual (Present), or Past, Grand Officers. Where a Brother is of higher rank than an office he holds, use the modes of address for the higher rank.

It is enough to address the Brother occupying the Chair without adding names, titles, office and rank of all the Brethren of rank. The indication given in speeches, "W.M. and Brethren," suffices except in special circumstances, as, for instance, where a Brother is being specially addressed for taking part in the proceedings, and is the only Brother referred to. (See Speech No. 73, second part.)

It would be well to familiarise yourself with the Titles and Precedence of Officers of Grand Lodge, Provincial and District Grand Lodges, as given in the Book of Constitutions, Articles 5 and 6, and as to other than Craft Degrees in the corresponding books.

———————

Generally speaking it is unnecessary to begin a speech by saying "Worshipful Master, Grand Officers, Provincial Grand Officers, and Brethren," the short form of "Worshipful Master and Brethren," or "Worshipful Master, Bro. Wardens and Brethren," is sufficient, the latter being a form which allows a courtesy compliment to be paid to the Wardens who, with the Master, form the three principal officers of the Lodge. In coupling the name of a brother with a toast, however, there is need to give the correct prefix. Thus, one should say, "I couple with this toast the name of Very Worshipful Bro. . . . . , or W. Bro. . . . . , or Bro. . . . . , as the case may be.

Prefixes and titles also enter the preparation of the menu card or programme or seating plan, and it should be observed that there is a correct way of designing Masonic titles. The letter "P" used as a prefix to a title indicates "Past," and care should be taken to see that it is not incorrectly used to designate a Provincial Grand Officer. Thus P.G.W. stands for Past Grand Warden of the United Grand Lodge of England, and not for Provincial Grand Warden. The latter should be designated thus : Prov. G.W. The Province may be indicated in brackets, thus : Prov. G.W. (Herts.) if desired. The title for a Past Provincial Grand Warden would be indicated by P. Prov. G.W.

When a brother has a civil title as well as Masonic titles, the modes of address or of printing the name would become, for example, W. Bro. Sir Edward . . . . , P.G.D.

Although the Master can generally depend upon Bro. Director of Ceremonies to advise him if necessary concerning the order of precedence of Grand Lodge Officers and other distinguished visitors, it would be well for the Master to become somewhat familiar with the matter himself by studying Article 5 of the Book of Constitutions.

27

USEFUL PHRASES AND QUOTATIONS FOR MASONIC AFTER-DINNER SPEECHES

FREEMASONRY is more than the art of learning the ritual, it is the science of living.

———

The effect of Freemasonry upon personal character can be judged by the attributes of members of the Craft in other spheres, i.e., as citizens, and as contributors to the well-being of a locality, state or nation.

———

The Craft can be in no danger of lapsing from power through a decline in numbers, neither need it fear external enemies, its principal danger being that its own members may lose sight of its true nature or its ancient ideals.

———

A good Mason represents manhood at its best.

———

Saved pennies make men rich, but pennies saved for the Masonic Institutions make Masons happy.

———

Brotherly love implies that kindness, one thread of which binds more surely than bands of steel.

———

Even junior officers should realise that it is a great thing to do a little thing well.

———

The experience of centuries lies behind the traditions of the Craft.

———

All Past Masters were once Entered Apprentices.

Welcome is that visitor who appreciates another's hospitality and aims.

————

Masonic life is a measure to be filled, not a cup to be drained.

————

Self-help is the root of all genuine growth in the individual, and the Mason who reads, helps himself.

————

Masonic gentility is the ability to ignore in others those faults or blemishes we would not tolerate in ourselves.

————

Many a father fails to realise how little he knows until he has to help a child with his homework. Likewise many a Master Mason only realises the limit of his Masonic knowledge when faced with the questions of an Entered Apprentice.

————

It is easy to be generous when affluent, but it is going without to give that builds character.

————

The visitor who is welcomed in the ante-room by others than the brother who invited him feels that he is a member of a real fraternity.

————

Let the nature of the effort be the gauge by which we measure the success of others. Judge them not altogether by the result of their efforts, for some may have striven with all their might and main yet have failed to attain success.

————

The real principles of Masonry are to be found in the hearts of men, not in the form of badges on a watch-chain.

Masonry is substantially the same the world over. The same can be said of music, and like music, Masonry speaks with a different voice to every hearer. To the student its utterances are most profound ; to the religious it is a voice from the altar ; to both it is harmony.

———

But strew his ashes to the wind
Whose sword or voice has served mankind.
And he is dead, whose glorious mind
    Lifts thine on high ?
To live in hearts we leave behind
    Is not to die.

———

We cannot all be famous, but we can all contribute toward the common weal, and our energies so put forth, reflect on others just as the moon reflects the sun's ray at eventide.

———

"Be very cautious whom you recommended as a candidate for initiation ; one false step on this point may be fatal. If you introduce a disputatious person, confusion will be produced, which may end in the dissolution of the Lodge." —DR. OLIVER.

———

"Our object is not so much to get more men into Freemasonry, as to get more Masonry into men."—DR. CHARLES JOHNSON.

———

"When I first determined to link myself with this noble Institution, it was a matter of very serious consideration with me, and I can assure the brethren that it was at a period when, at least, I had the power of well considering the matter, for it was not in the boyish days of my youth, but at the more mature age of twenty-five or twenty-six years. I did not take it up as a light and trivial matter, but as a grave and serious concern of my life. I worked may way diligently, passing through all the different offices of Junior and Senior Warden, Master of a Lodge, then Deputy Grand Master, until I finally closed it by the proud station which I have now the honour to hold. Therefore, having studied it, having reflected upon it, I know the value of the Institution ; and, may I venture to say, that, in all my transactions through life, the rules and principles laid down and prescribed by our Order have been to the best of my faculties strictly followed. And if I have been of use to Society at large, it must be attributed, in a great degree, to the impetus derived from Masonry."—H.R.H. THE DUKE OF SUSSEX. G.M. 1813-1843.

———

"A good Secretary is the backbone of a Lodge, even if the Master is nothing but a wishbone."—H. E. COOKE.

———

"What greater 'League of Nations' can be conceived, what more potent factor for peace, what greater honour than to be made a Freemason ?"—A. W. G. SCHEY.

———

"Learn all the lessons the Craft can teach you ; veiled in allegory they may be, but look around, there are the symbols to illustrate the story. Do not be content to be merely a member of a Lodge—be a Mason."—A. W. G. SCHEY.

———

"It had sometimes been claimed that the boys (at the R.M.I.B.) were perhaps better educated at Bushey than if their fathers had been alive ; but whilst this need not necessarily be true, the best we could give them was not too good."—W. A. STERLING.

"Perhaps no tenderer sentiment is to be found in all Masonry than that which clings about our Mother Lodge. For most of us, at least, the Lodge where we were raised stands out above all others with a peculiar radiance. She may be small, she may be weak, she may be tucked away in a little country town, she may have no distinguished sons to the Masonic or political world, and yet—she raised us ! It was in her sacred portals that we first saw Masonic light. It was through her that we were taken for ever from the plane on which we moved and had our being, and lifted to the Masonic level, given millions of brethren to call on in time of need, millions of opportunities to answer a call should it come . . .   Many a man absent from home for a protracted period has found the visit in the foreign Jurisdiction a cure for homesickness, but never a Brother who loves his Masonic Mother who can visit a Lodge away from home and not be a little homesick !"—D. WRIGHT.

"Masonry is not always on trial, but Masons are."—JUDGE GRAM.

"Freemasons should ever remember the purpose to which they are committed, that this fraternity to which they have given their allegiance is founded upon eternal principles of truth, that it is designed to be the great moral force of the age for breaking down the barriers which separate men from each other, and for the creation of charity as broad as the race."—A GRAND OFFICER.

"That man has a Masonic heart who can sympathise with men in their sorrow and even in their sins, who when he makes friends keeps them, who loves flowers and children, and can hunt birds without a gun, who can respond to the cry of distress and who can enjoy the laugh of a child, who can look into the face of a forlorn soul and see something beside sin."—C. GRAYSON.

"When in trouble or difficulty, and your heart is aching for some kindly gesture or sympathy, here is a Brother who, with no apparent sense of superiority, comes and greets you in that fraternal brotherly spirit that makes you feel instantly the reality of his friendship ; when through nervousness or faulty memory you stumble in the ceremonial work of the Lodge, Bro. Greatheart never reproaches you, but with his cheery words and kindly look enheartens you."—X.Y.Z.

"Orpheus taught the worship of combined harmony, aspiring to the Deity by means of musical chords. The pupils were then told to 'tyle' against false notes. Each pupil would then sound a separate note on his lute, endeavouring to harmonise with his master in building a column of music that would inspire the whole. As the musician tries everything on his instrument, so the W.M. sounds every officer at his post and reminds all brethren of their 'constant care'."—B. Tullues.

"The greatness, power and reality of our Brotherhood is that we are bound together in the service of God, and humanity, and its charity is not confined to giving aid to the needy and distressed, but embraces the broader view of exemplifying the true fraternal duties and obligations man owes to man."—C. Grayson.

"Masonry is a sacramental system, possessing, like all sacraments, an outward and visible side consisting of its ceremonial, its doctrine, and its symbols which we can see and hear, and an inward intellectual and spiritual side, which is concealed behind the ceremonial, the doctrine and the symbols, and which is available only to the Mason who has learned to use his spiritual imagination and who can appreciate the reality that lies behind the veil of outward symbol."—W. L. Wilmshurst.

"I cannot too strongly impress upon you, brethren, the fact that, throughout our rituals and our lectures, the references made to the Lodge are *not* to the building in which we meet. That building itself is intended to be but a symbol, a veil of allegory concealing something else. 'Know ye not,' says the great initiate, St. Paul, 'that ye are the temples of the Most High ; and that the spirit of God dwelleth in you ?' The real Lodge referred to throughout our rituals is our own individual personalities, and if we interpret our doctrine in light of this fact, we shall find that it reveals an entirely new aspect of our Craft."—W. L. WILMSHURST.

———

"At the centre of ourselves, deeper than any dissecting-knife can reach or than any physical investigation can fathom, lies buried the 'vital and immortal principle,' the 'glimmering ray' that affiliates us to the Divine Centre of all life, and that is never wholly extinguished, however imperfect our lives may be."—W. L. WILMSHURST.

———

"The Craft that in 1721 was so signally advanced by the accession to its ranks of the Duke of Montague has since then shown itself to be a force that is independent of and superior to all social distinctions, all external advantages of rank and fortune. To-day it still asks of its members only that they shall be well and worthily recommended and desirous to render themselves more serviceable to their fellow-creatures."—L. VIBERT.

———

"The exact course of development by which the one simple ceremony of early operative days expanded into three degrees cannot be stated with confidence, and has been the subject of a whole literature of its own. At all events, by 1723 in England, there were two ceremonies recognised. One was the apprentices' ceremony and the other the Master's Part. By 1731 there were three, but their exact relation to the previous two is not clear. It seems probable from a consideration of the ceremonies themselves and on other grounds that the apprentice degree was split into two the second being the Fellow Craft. We probably still have to-day a very close approximation to the three degrees as they then stood."—L. VIBERT.

———

"It was the custom at the Shakespeare's Head Lodge, and among the higher class Lodges of olden times for members and visitors to entertain the brethren at the various meetings by giving lectures or readings."—H. SADLER.

———

"If Masonry be truly lived and faithfully exemplified, it never casts a shadow upon a home, never wounds a human heart or wrongs a human soul. It is ever sensitive to the cry of the needy and responsive to the wants of the deserving. It may be regarded as one of the mighty forces of to-day working for the uplifting of society."—REV. JOSEPH JOHNSON.

———

"It is when Freemasonry is taken seriously by sincere and honest men that ennoblement of life begins. By giving a new zest to duty, it creates a truer sense of the relations between man and man."—REV. JOSEPH JOHNSON.

———

"Without charity, eloquence is meaningless, knowledge is empty, and sacrifice is fruitless. Our gifts must be symbols of brotherhood and the visible expression of our sympathy . . . Consider the deep concern the Craft has for the aged who have outlived active service . . . No longer able to maintain themselves they are treated not as mendicants, but as living members of our great Brotherhood."—REV. JOSEPH JOHNSON.

"It is to the spread of the spirit and practice of Masonry, making alike for international and industrial peace, that civilisation may look for the best pledge of restoring tranquillity to a distracted world."—SIR JOHN A. COCKBURN.

———

God bless thy year—
   Thy coming in, thy going out,
The rest, thy travelling about,
   The rough, the smooth, the bright, the drear,
God bless thy year.

BROWNING

———

"Blessed is the man who having nothing to say abstains from giving us wordy evidence of the fact."—GEORGE ELLIOT.

———

"The greatest art of all has been said to be the art of living. It has also been said to be the art of giving. Surely these two statements are complementary for we are only living to the extent that we can give, whether it be in money, time, service, or cheerful inspiration.

———

Human beings, like plants, flourish if sunshine sometimes follows rain, and if praise occasionally follows criticism.

———

Masonry teaches the relative importance of self-analysis to the duties of life. If each day or night you review your actions, behaviour and thoughts, and try to see how they coincide with your own philosophy, and measure up to the standards outlined in the Craft, you will be improving yourself as a man and a brother.

———

The pessimist looks at his glass and cries "My glass is half empty," while the optimist looking at his glass, says "My glass is half full."

"An inspired and inspiring dedication to service should be part of every Mason's life. As expressed in such terms as relief to indigent and aged members, widows and orphans, the Craft has done and is doing magnificent work. But there is another half of Brotherhood that relief does not express. I refer to more intangible things—to that relation with our fellow members that calls out all the kindliness, tolerance and sympathy that we are capable of. Honest differences of opinion on policies of Lodge life may probably exist, but not suspicion and enmities."—C. H. JOHNSON.

———

Masonically we are heirs of the past. Masonry has come down to us in varying forms, sometimes along a way that has been a rough and difficult road. Our Masonic ancestors gave the Craft devotion, loyalty and faith, and made its name illustrious among institutions of the world. Ours is the responsibility to appreciate and to conserve the rich inheritance passed on to us by our forbears. Well may we say "Hats off to the past," but at the same time let us be willing to pursue the command, "Coats off to the future."

———

> To hold you in perpetual amity,
> To make you brother and to knit your hearts
> With an unspilling knot.
>
> SHAKESPEARE

———

> That you may keep th' unerring line,
> Still rising by the plummet's law,
> Till order bright completely shine,
> Shall be my pray'r when far awa.
>
> BURNS

———

In your happiness remember others.

———

No one receives as much as he who gives first.

Young man, said a father to his son, it is better to be silent and be thought a fool, than to speak inopportunely and at length, and leave the issue beyond doubt.

———

Benevolence is a word which implies that none of us prosper but by the Grace of God, and that there is a duty to see that those who need are provided for. Nature provided the dew ponds of Chantonbury Ring and other places that young lambs might not die of thirst, and these ponds have never been known to dry up. May the spring of benevolence in the Craft never be known to dry up also.

———

"Think what could have been done by Masonry, through Masonry, for all the world."—KIPLING.

———

Truth is within ourselves.
It takes no rise
From outward things, whate'er you may believe,
There is an inmost centre in ourselves
Where truth abides in fullness, and to know
Rather consists in finding out a way
Whence this imprisoned splendour may escape,
Than by effecting entrance for a light
Supposed to be without.

———

At the time when the fortunes of war weighed heavily and we were almost downcast with despair, as Britain, unprepared, stood alone to fight a ruthless enemy, His Majesty the King used a quotation, till then hardly known.

"And I said to the man at the gate of the year : 'Give me a light that I may tread safely into the unknown.' And he replied, 'Go out into the darkness and put thine hand into the Hand of God. This shall be to thee better than light and safer than a known way'."

In that quotation lies the philosophy of our faith and belief in Him who has guided our destinies, and in the fulfilment of which may we hope to rebuild a civilisation stronger and better—one in which the great Masonic principles of brotherly love and universal peace will ever prevail.

———

Bason, in one of his essays, laid it down that friendship saved us from solitude, and strengthened us with a faithful ally. To-day, we are largely a world of town dwellers, and perhaps there is no one so lonely as the town dweller, surrounded by so many, yet knowing so few. Freemasonry provides us with an opportunity of gaining friends, not only in our own Lodge, but in the Lodges we visit, and gives men a common interest upon which many a casual meeting has developed into a life-long and close friendship.

———

Masonry is worth to us all that we are worth to it— neither more nor less. Many complain that there is nothing in Masonry, forgetting that they have put nothing into it. If we really absorb its teachings and obey its tenets, it cannot be otherwise than of great benefit to us, as it has been to hundreds who have gone before us.

———

Our ancient Brotherhood is founded upon the principles of love, hope and charity—principles that through many centuries have led to the betterment of mankind. In Masonry one should be taught to search not for transient pleasure, but for a philosophy, for guidance that will aid him to gain the most from the short time accorded here, by contributing the most to his fellow man.

Bro. J. H. COWLES.

———

Freemasonry lives to help and helps men to live.

It has been a distinct pleasure to visit this Lodge because my host, Bro. ————, has often discussed the Craft with me, and I have been particularly impressed by the fact that in referring to this Lodge he always used the pronoun "We". We do this, we did that, we are a founding Lodge, etc. Never did he refer to it as "My" Lodge, this indicating that the corporate spirit had been well developed in your Lodge, a point on which I am reassured after having had the pleasure of joining in your assembly.

> I pray the prayer that the Easterns do.
> May the love of Allah abide with you ;
> Wherever you are, wherever you go,
> May the beautiful palms of Allah grow,
> In days of labour and nights of rest,
> May the love of Allah make you blest,
> So I touch my heart as the Easterns do,
> May the peace of Allah abide with you.

When I was young in the Craft all the P.M.s seemed to be very old, very important and very austere. Now that I am one myself and I look around, they all seem very young, very ordinary, and very approachable.

Neither a Mason nor a W.M. should be judged solely by the results of his labours. He might strive with all his heart and all his strength, yet not be entirely successful in comparison with one to whom certain things came easily. Masonry teaches us to try, to make an effort, and the amount of effort should be the gauge by which to determine the result.

Your visitors, in common with your members, will leave to-night refreshed and better for having been impressed within the Lodge by the tenets of the Craft and spirit of brotherhood which prevailed. They will be the stronger for having, for a brief space of time, been freed from the rivalries of business, the bitterness of political life, the jealousies of mankind, and the jarring sounds of the outside world with all its petty troubles and squabbles.

———

Sir Frederick Bramwell, a distinguished scientist, when attending a dinner to celebrate the 600th Anniversary of Peterhouse College, rising to reply to the toast of "Applied Science" at 11 p.m., said that "at that hour of the night the only application of science which seemed to him at all relevant would be the application of the domestic lucifer to the bedroom candle". Likewise, I feel that, at this late hour, it would be unkind for a visitor to keep his hosts up longer by making a lengthy speech worthy of the hospitality the visitors have received.

———

Ben Tillett said, "Friendship is above price. Wherever it is found in reality, you find beauty and goodness and love. It helps men to forgive—even to forgive themselves— and to forget the sins of others as well as their own. It is the lack of friendship from which the world is suffering to-day." These words came back to me as I was thinking during the evening what a wonderful opportunity lay before our Craft in fostering friendship between men to the fullest extent, an idea prompted by the genial atmosphere of your assembly and evident spirit of goodwill that pervades your Lodge.

28

CONCLUSION

SO must come to an end this volume concerning a subject on which hundreds of pages might well be written, and perhaps no more fitting conclusion to a book of this character can be found than the following quotation from a speech delivered by a Master of the Author's Lodge :—

(175) "Charles Lamb once remarked : 'Sentimentally I am disposed to harmony, but organically I am incapable of a tune.' In like manner, by inclination I would be an orator, but temperamentally I am prone to silence. In these circumstances what was to be done ? By fortunate chance, I recalled that that great master of prose and poetry, Alexander Pope, laid it down that, 'True ease in writing comes from art, not chance.' Why not apply this to Masonic Speech-making ? It therefore occurred to me that the one thing to do during my Mastership was to use one's art, and not trust to chance. By this means one might succeed in satisfying the cravings of the Brethren of the Author's Lodge for speeches which on the one hand would not unduly interfere with the functioning of the digestive organs, and on the other, might not disgrace one's learned predecessors. Incidentally, as results of one's experience, if one may presume to advise any budding Masonic speaker, I would say : (1) Concentrate more on Freemasonry and what it means, and less on fulsome compliments ; and (2) turn over the pages of a few more books. By so doing, you may succeed in saying something which is not usually said and thus earn the respect, if not the gratitude, of your brethren and fellows."